A Copyright Sampler

CJCLS Guide #2

Edited by

Wanda K. Johnston
Central Florida Community College
Ocala, Florida

Derrie B. Roark
Hillsborough Community College
Tampa, Florida

Community and Junior College Libraries Section
Association of College and Research Libraries
A Division of the American Library Association
Chicago 1996

The paper used in this publication meets the minimum requirements of American National Standard for Information Sciences–Permanence of Paper for Printed Library Materials, ANSI Z39.48-1992. ∞

Library of Congress Cataloging-in-Publication Data
A copyright sampler / edited by Wanda K. Johnston, Derrie B. Roark.
     p.   cm. -- (CJCLS guide ; #2)
  Includes bibliographical references and index.
  ISBN 0-8389-7878-9 (alk. paper)
  1. Fair use (Copyright)--United States. 2. Academic libraries--Law and legislation--United States. 3. College librarians--United States--Handbooks, manuals, etc. 4. Copyrights--United States--Forms. I. Johnston, Wanda K. II. Roark, Derrie B.
III. Association of College and Research Libraries. Community and Junior College Libraries Section. IV. Series.
KF3030.1.Z9C66 1996
346.7304'82--dc21   96-51467

Printed in the United States of America.

00 99 98 97 96   5 4 3 2 1 ·

CONTENTS

INTRODUCTION

The foundation of the copyright law in the United States can be traced to England and the 1710 Statute of Queen Anne. The initial questioning of who has rights to what has been written began with the printing press; the Statute of Queen Anne gave rights to the author, not to the printer, and recognized "that the best means of encouraging creativity was to grant authors the right to the fruits of their labor." (Bielefield, 27)

American copyright law has its roots in the Constitution, specifically the clause referred to as the Copyright-Patent Clause, "The Congress shall have Power ... To promote the Progress of Science and useful Arts, by securing for limited Times to Authors and Inventors the exclusive Right to their respective Writings and Discoveries." (Article I, Section 8, Clause 8 of the U.S. Constitution) Congress must foster creativity and protect the rights of the creators, while not curtailing the production of "raw materials" needed for new creations. As James Boyle so aptly wrote, " An intellectual property system has to insure that the fertile public domain is not converted into a fallow landscape of walled plots." (Boyle, 10)

While the struggles with the 1976 copyright law and its amendments continue, the bottom line is that it is illegal to violate any of the rights extended to the owner of the copyright. However, these rights are not unlimited. The Copyright Law, Title 17, U.S. Code, and related guidelines, basically address the issue of who has the right to copy. The only obvious answer is that the owner of the copyright has the right to copy. Anyone else must request permission to copy, or must fall under sections of the law which grant such privileges.

Educational institutions are afforded many privileges not available to the general public. Most of these are found in Sections 106 to 110 and concern fair use, electronic databases, photocopying, interlibrary loan, and public performance. But the issues of copyright are not limited to libraries. College bookstores, dorms, student activities, instructional services, and production facilities all have responsibilities to address copyright.

One of the best ways to address copyright is to do so collegewide. Institutional policies and procedures approved by the college president and the college board of directors/trustees, followed up with publications and training, could play a vital role in keeping an institution out of the middle of copyright violations. The library/learning resources program must take obvious steps to protect itself and the institution; but the library/learning resources program can provide a major service to the institution by initiating drafts of policies and procedures for other areas of the institution as well.

With college commitment, procedures, training, and coordination, the institution should find that almost anything that a faculty member or student wants to do in the classroom or for research is available through the Law and/or its related guidelines. If a faculty member needs something quickly, there is a great likelihood that it is available for him to copy; if he has more lead time, there is no excuse not to request permission to use the item. With the technologies afforded to institutions, many requests for permission can be handled through a phone call, a fax request, or an e-mail message. Turnaround time can be amazing. Of course, there are always those items that are difficult to track down and there will be occasional denials, but the requesting process shows much good faith and the effort should be rewarded. Besides obvious calls, messages, or letters to publishers or distributors, there are services available which assist institutions, libraries, and individuals with copyright registrations, permissions, and inquiries. Again, there is no reason today to break the law.

Lastly, consider the ethical issues involved with copyright and intellectual property. The old adage, "Do unto others as you want done to you," works very well in understanding copyright. Much creativity comes from our institutions of higher learning; we build on each others creations. As wisely said by Northrop Frye, "Poetry can only be made out of other poems; novels out of other novels." We must treat each others creations with the respect with which we would like our own to be treated. And we must take seriously the task of "role model" as we stand before our students and our users. We must speak out against copyright violations and for the respect of intellectual property just as we would speak out against censorship and for academic/intellectual freedom.

This publication will supply its owner with samples of copyright policies, procedures, and publications. You, as the owner of a copy of this publication, have permission to use the published documents as samples to write your own policies and procedures for your institution and library/learning resources program. The suppliers of the documents have also agreed to be contacted to answer any questions you may have regarding their documents. This publication should in no way replace the legal advice you can be afforded by your college attorney. However, we hope that it will help you assist your institution in understanding what it can do to protect itself from copyright violation.

References:

Bielefield, Arlene, and Lawrence Cheeseman. Libraries & Copyright Law. New York: Neal-Schuman, 1993.

Boyle, James. "Commentary: Sold Out." In Computers in Libraries 16 (May 1996): 8,10.

SURVEY REVIEW

The inception of this project occurred when the two editors compared their experiences as Copyright Officers for their respective institutions. Both had been involved in developing board approved copyright policies, drafting informational documents and signs, as well as conducting institutional copyright workshops. Based upon their experience and the cooperative nature of library/learning resources personnel, they agreed that a "sampler" of copyright materials might be useful for those who are facing the challenge of creating formal copyright policies, procedures, and publications and for those who are reviewing and updating their existing copyright materials.

HISTORY

This manual is the second in the CJCLS Guide Series, following the popular Collection Management in the Electronic Age. The Guide Series grew out of the CJCLS Research and Publications Committee, chaired by Beverley Gass of Guilford Technical Community College (NC). The committee's goal is to encourage and sponsor ALA publications relating directly to two-year academic institutions. The series is modeled after the ACRL CLIP Notes. With Beverley's assistance, the editors were granted funding for the project through the ACRL New Publications Committee.

In February 1996, the "CJCLS Survey of Copyright Policies and Practices" (see Appendix) was mailed to 310 members of the Community and Junior College Libraries Section. Care was taken to send to only one person per institution. After the April 1 response deadline, a reminder was posted on the CJC-L listserve inviting anyone who had not responded to please do so and anyone wishing to participate who had not been contacted to respond. By June 1, eighty librarians, or 26% of those surveyed, returned useable completed surveys.

The editors were initially concerned by the low rate of return until one librarian pointed out the sensitive nature of copyright as a topic: "If a document was shared with any inaccuracies, could their institution be liable for the misinformation or subject to prosecution for non-compliance with the law?" Thus, although the contributors to this sampler have granted permission to owners of this publication to use these documents as examples as they write their own policies and procedures, the editors emphasize that these examples should not replace legal advice. The purpose of this sampler is not to provide legal documents but instead to encourage copyright compliance.

SURVEY SUMMARY

Survey respondents represent a range of institution sizes. Approximately half of the library/learning resources departments are in institutions with fewer than 3000 full-time equivalent students and have fewer than ten full-time staff. Fifty three (66%) of the eighty institutions represented have formal written copyright policies. Of the fifty-three, forty (61%) have institution-wide policies, eleven (17%) have Library/Learning Resources Department policies, and four (.5%) have policies for specific services. Of the fifty-three, 25 (38%) had the institution-wide copyright policy endorsed or adopted by Board of Trustees action, 16 (24%) by administrative procedure, and 14 (21%) by library/learning resources procedure. In addition to this sampler, Charles Vlcek's Adoptable Copyright Policy provides guidance with the creation of an institutional policy and informational guide.

Nearly every respondent uses separate written copyright procedures or forms for services. As might be expected, most have copyright procedures and forms for interlibrary loan (43%), library reserves (34%), and off-air video copying (32%). Somewhat fewer responded with procedures for computer software/database use (25%), the copy center/duplication (25%), and media production/adaptation (21%). The Appendix includes the text of the fair use criteria as well as related copyright guidelines for specific services.

Forty-two respondents (53%) indicated that no one person holds responsibility for institutional copyright issues. Seventeen (21%) stated that the responsibility was assigned to the Director of Learning Resources. Other individuals named as responsible were deans of instruction, deans of students, or deans of administration, the public information officer, the college attorney, the director of media services, or a copyright committee.

Faculty and staff learn about copyright through written informational booklets (50%), workshops (31%), forms (25%), news stories (21%), and electronic/Internet resources (15%). Other sources of copyright information include administrative procedures, newsletters and memos, informal consultation or librarian assistance, signs, faculty handbooks, and journal articles. Janis Bruwelheide's The Copyright Primer for Librarians and Educators was frequently cited for its usefulness. This primer's appendices include the text of sections 106-110 of the copyright law, Internet resources, and sources of further assistance, e.g. the Copyright Clearance Center and the Television Licensing Center. Rosemary Talab's Copyright and Instructional Technologies was often suggested as a guide for media and technology copyright issues. Both books include practical question and answer sections. Arlene Bielefield and Lawrence Cheesman's Libraries & Copyright Law includes a useful section on required library copyright notices. A selective bibliography is included in the Appendix of this copyright sampler.

In addition, a plethora of explanations and interpretations of copyright exist in other resources found on-line. The United Stated Copyright Office makes available frequently requested Copyright Office circulars, announcements, and the most recent proposed as well as final regulations through its website at *http://lcweb.loc.gov/copyright*. This site also provides links to copyright resources created elsewhere. California State University, State University of New York, and City University of New York jointly represent the Consortium for Educational Technology for University Systems which produced an informational guide entitled, "Fair Use of Copyrighted Works: A Crucial Element in Educating America." An electronic version of this guide is available on the home page of the Consortium at *http://www.cetus.org*. The Consortium grants permission to reproduce and distribute copies of its publication, provided that copies are distributed at or below cost, that the source is credited, and that its copyright notice is included on each copy. In addition, the Consortium maintains a listserve at *fairuse-talk-request@calstate.edu*. The Music Library Association sponsors a web site at *http://www.music.indiana.edu/tech_s/mla/index.htm* to help librarians make better informed decisions regarding music copyright issues.

BOARD POLICIES

The Board approved copyright policy formally states the Board's intention to observe the copyright law and to establish institution-wide procedures for ensuring copyright compliance. Failure to adopt and support an institutional copyright policy places the Board in jeopardy if the institution is sued for copyright infringement due to the illegal actions of employees. Vlcek's Adoptable Copyright Policy suggests that the copyright policy include the following components:

1. A statement that the Board intends to abide by the Copyright Law and related guidelines;
2. A statement prohibiting copying not specifically permitted by the law, fair use, license agreement, or the permission of the copyright holder;
3. A statement placing the liability for willful infringement upon the person making or requesting the copy;
4. A statement naming a copyright officer for the institution;
5. A statement mandating appropriate notices on or near all equipment capable of making copies;
6. A statement requiring record retention of all copyright permissions and license agreements;
7. A statement requiring an informational publication detailing what copying can and cannot be done by employees.

Fifty three (66%) of the survey respondents indicated that they do have a formal written copyright policy. Of these, forty have institution-wide policies with 38%

approved by board action. In other instances, copyright policy was set forth through administrative procedure (24%) and library/learning resources department procedure (21%).

The Board Policy section presents exemplary policies shared by survey respondents. The Clackamas Community College copyright policy is succinct and when paired with its corresponding administrative regulation incorporates all seven suggested components of a board policy. Hillsborough Community College Board approved the Copyright Law Compliance as an administrative rule supplemented by a number of specific administrative procedures, e.g. copyright officer. Of special note is the requirement that "faculty and student association advisors will advise students and student government associations regarding the use of copyrighted materials outside of the classroom." The Montgomery College policy on the Use of Copyrighted Materials specifies the expectations of the Board and authorizes the President to establish implementation procedures. Kirtland Community College combined informational guidelines into its board policy. The University of Colorado at Denver's Auraria Library incorporates informational guidelines into its Board policy.

INFORMATIONAL DOCUMENTS

Once a copyright policy which clearly delineates rationale and procedures is adopted, faculty and staff must learn about these copyright issues. Vlcek suggests that an informational publication be created introducing copyright and detailing what copying can and cannot be done. Among the survey respondents, forty (50%) indicated that they learned about copyright issues through written informational booklets. While many respondents included examples of copyright documents prepared for their faculty and staff, others shared their own preferred copyright resources, e.g. Bruwelheide's The Copyright Primer. The Consortium for Educational Technology for University Systems developed an excellent joint publication, "Fair Use of Copyrighted Works: A Crucial Element in Educating America," which is available on the home page of the Consortium (http://www.cetus.org). Permission is granted for the reproduction and distribution of this publication for nonprofit educational purposes, provided that the distribution is at or below cost, that the source is cited, and that a copyright notice is included on each copy.

Other methods of disseminating information to faculty and staff about copyright included workshops (31%), forms (25%), news stories (21%), electronic/Internet resources (15%), and other methods (30%), such as administrative procedures, newsletters and memos, signs, faculty handbooks, and informal consultation.

The Informational Documents section features complete instructional publications focusing on copyright developed by Pikes Peak Community College, Broome Community College, and Tallahassee Community College. Pima Community College and Chattanooga State Technical Community College summarize this information in three-fold copyright brochures. Manatee Community College inserts "Copyright Policies" in its campus telephone directory. This practice ensures that every employee has copyright information readily available in perhaps the most frequently used campus document.

Edmonds Community College has established "Copyright Centers" at various institution locations. These centers are described as physical places "where faculty and staff in your area can access the information and materials they need to understand and follow copyright policies, procedures, and guidelines." Each center includes The Copyright Primer, the college copyright policy, supporting procedures/guidelines handouts, and a copyright orientation video. Faculty and staff are encouraged to direct questions to the Director of Learning Resources.

SPECIFIC APPLICATIONS

Nearly every institution has separate written copyright procedures and/or forms for specific service applications. Most prevalent were interlibrary loan (43%), library reserves (34%), and off-air video copying (32%). Other applications included computer software/databases (25%), copy center/print duplication (25%), media production/adaptation (21%), and music performance rights (13%). Brief mention was also made of publications center, college bookstore, and electronic information transmission applications.

The Specific Applications section includes sample procedures and forms for interlibrary loan, library reserves, photocopied materials and course packets, video viewing and off-air taping, media adaptation and production, instructional ITV use, music and fair use, and computer applications. While many institutions contributed sample forms and procedures relating to a wide variety of service applications, the editors noted as most prevalent the copyright treatment of more traditional applications, such as library reserves, interlibrary loan, etc. Among the more unique copyright treatments is the University of Maine at Augusta/Education Network of Maine with its ITV policy for distance learning. North Country Community College provides sample off-air broadcasting forms as well as addresses for obtaining permissions to its informational guide. Northwest Michigan College incorporates a "Primer on Distance Learning and Intellectual Property Issues" by Kenneth D. Salomon of Dow, Lohnes & Albertson into their distance learning/interactive television training guide. Dow, Lohnes & Albertson serves as legal counsel to the American Association of Community Colleges with special emphasis on the issue of intellectual property policies for community colleges with distance learning. The firm maintains various articles on intellectual property policy on its website located at *http://www.dla.com/education/index2.html*.

Austin Community College shares information about copyright through a series of flyers on various aspects of copyright. "Music and Fair Use" and "Computer Software and Fair Use" are included in this sampler. Kirkwood Community College has developed a Board policy and guidelines for responsible use of the College's computing resources. Hillsborough Community College treats specific copyright applications through a series of related administrative procedures. William Rainey Harper College uses a standard form for obtaining rights to closed caption video acquisitions. The Pennsylvania College of Technology clarifies ownership of copyrighted materials developed by college employees through a policy statement.

FACTORS AFFECTING COPYRIGHT AND THE FUTURE

The low rate of return from this survey may indicate the sensitive nature of copyright and the lack of institutional policy regarding copyright. One librarian was concerned about sharing her institutional policies and procedures due to a concern that they might not meet public review. A Director of Learning Resources indicated that he has been trying for years to get a policy commitment from the institution, to no avail. Indeed, some institutions seem hesitant to develop policy or have not found it a worthwhile task; yet, copyright authorities continue to emphasize that policy, procedure, and information sharing demonstrate good faith efforts for institutions to avoid litigation.

As indicated by the survey response, those institutions that have addressed copyright have focused on the more traditional aspects of copyright, e.g. interlibrary loan, library reserves, and off-air taping. Fewer respondents focused on copyright issues surrounding electronic databases, Internet usage, multimedia production, and the transmission of live classroom activity via distance learning technology. As institutions provide more information access through on-line services and other newer technologies, copyright interpretation will become more complex and understanding of related guidelines will become even more essential for administrators, librarians, faculty, and students.

BOARD POLICIES

Clackamas Community College
Hillsborough Community College
Montgomery College
Kirtland Community College
University of Colorado at Denver

TITLE: COPYRIGHT POLICY   Policy 719

The Board of Education declares that the policy of Clackamas Community College is to adhere to the provisions of the US Copyright Law (Title 17, United States Code, Section 101, et seq). Although there continues to be controversy regarding interpretation of the copyright law, this policy represents a sincere effort to operate legally. The Board directs the administration to provide college employees, contractors, and students with guidelines that clearly discourage violation of copyright law.

Directives on the implementation of copyright compliance are contained in the college Administrative Regulations. Comprehensive information about copyright rules is published in the Copyright Manual for Clackamas Community College, available to all college employees through their division office or the Office of Human Resources.

CCC Board Policy Manual
Updated July 1994
Approved by Board August 3, 1994

Clackamas Community College

ADMINISTRATIVE REGULATION

AR 2-22-91-0021

SUBJECT: COPYRIGHT COMPLIANCE

1. CCC prohibits, on the part of its employees, contractors, or students, copying not specifically allowed by the federal copyright law, fair use guidelines, license agreements or copyright owner's permission. This prohibition applies to all media holding copyrights including print, music, computer software, audio-visual media, etc.

2. Any individual employed or contracted by CCC who infringes the copyright law as specifically prohibited by CCC policy, may be subject to individual legal prosecution. If actions by individuals involve the college's legal liability, and it is determined that the individual willfully disregarded the law and CCC policy, such an individual may be subject to college disciplinary measures.

3. CCC shall appoint the Dean of Instruction as Copyright Officer and grant such Officer the authority to develop and implement policy; serve as liaison with legal counsel,; and provide information and training to employees about policy and copyright issues.

4. A copyright manual shall be developed to address copyright issues relevant to CCC. The manual shall be regularly updated and distributed to all CCC employees, at the direction of the Copyright Officer.

5. In compliance with Section 108 of the U.S. Copyright Law, appropriate warning notices shall be placed on or near all equipment capable of duplicating copyrighted materials. Copying devices include, but are not limited to, photocopiers, offset presses, transparency makers, audio recorders, video recorders, and computers.

6. Copyright records, licenses and permissions shall be maintained under the supervision of the Copyright Officer.

Approved by President's Council 10/30/90.

L:\MISC\AR0021

Clackamas Community College

ADMINISTRATIVE RULES

Title: COPYRIGHT LAW COMPLIANCE	**Identification:** 6HX-10-3.010 **Page:** 1 of 1 **Effective Date:** June 17, 1992
Authority: SBE 6A-14.0262; 6A-14.0247 FS 240.319 Title 17 U.S. Code Sect. 101, et seq.	**Signature/Approval:** *[signature]*

PURPOSE

The purpose of this administrative rule is to establish College policy regarding the compliance of College employees and students to the U. S. Copyright Law and related guidelines.

RULE

Hillsborough Community College adheres to the provisions of the United States Copyright Law (Title 17, United States Code, Sect. 101, et. seq.) and to the fair use guidelines.

The College will establish a set of procedural guidelines to assist employees and students in adhering to those provisions. Furthermore, the College will provide an institutional program for informing and instructing all employees about the laws and its related guidelines.

College employees are expected to be familiar with the College's administrative copyright procedures currently in force under this rule. Furthermore, faculty and student association advisers will advise students and student government associations regarding the use of copyrighted materials outside of the classroom.

The College does not approve of any use or duplication of copyrighted materials not specifically allowed by the copyright law, fair use guidelines, license agreement, or the permission of the copyright owner.

ADMINISTRATIVE PROCEDURES

Title:	Identification: 3.500
COPYRIGHT COMPLIANCE:	Page: 1 of 2
COPYRIGHT OFFICER	Effective Date: September 15, 1992

Authority:	Signature/Approval:
SBE 6A-14.0262; 6A-14.0247 FS 240.319 Title 17 U.S. Code Sect. 101, et seq. 6HX-10-3.010	

PURPOSE

The purpose of this administrative procedure is to establish procedural guidelines regarding the copyright compliance policy of Hillsborough Community College. Copyright compliance refers to the use and duplication of any copyrighted material.

PROCEDURE

1. In order to adhere to the provisions of the U.S. Copyright Law (Title 17, U.S. Code, Section 101, et.seq.), Hillsborough Community College requires all faculty, staff, and administrators to follow copyright compliance procedures.

2. The Associate Vice President of Learning Resources Services will serve as the College's Copyright Officer and will be the contact for copyright policy questions and matters regarding use and duplication.   Questions concerning in-house publishing may be directed to the Bookstore Manager. When necessary, the Copyright Officer will consult with the College Attorney and/or other appropriate College employees, as well as outside copyright consultants.

3. The Copyright Officer will be responsible for developing, implementing, and maintaining copyright procedures and guidelines.

4. The Copyright Officer will be responsible for planning and implementing an institutional program to inform and instruct College employees regarding the provisions of the law and its related guidelines.

5. Copies of approved copyright procedures and guidelines will be distributed to faculty members and administrators, and will be available in the Learning Resources Center at each campus. College employees are expected to be familiar with the College's copyright compliance procedures.

ADMINISTRATIVE PROCEDURES

Identification:	Page:	Effective Date:
3.500	2 of 2	September 15, 1992

6. The Copyright Officer will provide appropriate warning notices, visible to persons using the equipment, which shall be placed on or near all equipment capable of making copies of copyrighted materials. Copying devices include photocopiers, mimeograph and ditto machines, transparency makers, audio recorders, video recorders, microform reader/printers, and computers.

7. The Copyright Officer will provide appropriate warning notices which shall be placed on software that might be copied, such as video tapes and audio tapes, and microcomputer software.

8. The Copyright Officer will maintain appropriate records regarding the use of copyrighted materials by employees. These records will include licenses, permissions, off-air duplicating, etc. When a College employee receives a permission, license, etc., it will be the responsibility of the employee to forward a copy of all relevant documents to the Copyright Officer. Exceptions must be discussed with and approved by the Copyright Officer.

POLICY Board of Trustees - Montgomery College   <u>68101</u>

Chapter: Fiscal and Administrative Affairs   Modification No.<u> 007 </u>

Subject: Use of Copyrighted Materials

- -

I.   The College recognizes that accomplishment of its mission may be facilitated by the use of works owned or created by others. It is the policy of the College that students, employees and other individuals who use College facilities and/or equipment, and students, employees, and other individuals who use off-campus non-College facilities and/or equipment in connection with College activities or on behalf of the College, shall recognize those accomplishments by respecting the intellectual property of others and using such works only to the extent such use would be permitted by law.

II.   This policy shall apply to students, employees, and other individuals who use College equipment and/or facilities and to students, employees, and other individuals who use off-campus non-College facilities and/or equipment in connection with College related activities or on behalf of the College. For example, this policy applies when photocopying is undertaken at a commercial copying center, at a self-service coin-operated machine in the library, or on any other reproduction equipment owned or leased by the College or used in connection with College activities or on behalf of the College.

III.   Students, employees and other individuals subject to this policy who use material originated by others shall not, as a matter of policy, when using such materials, infringe on those rights of the originator which are protected by copyright laws and shall secure permission to use or reproduce copyrighted works when such permission would be required under copyright law and/or pay royalties when such payment would be required. Students, employees and other individuals subject to this policy are expected to obtain permission from the copyright owners unless the intended use is clearly permitted under the doctrine of "fair use." Students, employees and other individuals subject to this policy are expected to be selective and sparing in copying.

IV.   "Fair Use" shall not be abused. The College does not condone copying instead of purchasing copyrighted works where such copying would constitute copyright infringement.

V.   For purposes of this policy copyrighted material means any work or intellectual property which may be subject to copyright under the laws of the United States. This includes but is not limited to literary works, including computer programs and compilations; musical works, including any accompanying words; dramatic works, including any accompanying music; pantomimes and choreographic works; pictorial, graphic, and sculptural works; motion pictures and other audiovisual works and sound recordings. For example, this policy applies to photocopying for classroom use, use of computer software, use of videocassettes, and off-air videotaping.

VI.   This policy is not intended to waive any rights, remedies, immunities or defenses available to the College in the event of an infringement or alleged infringement of the copyright law and such rights, remedies, immunities and defenses are specifically reserved.

VII.   The President is authorized to establish procedures to implement this policy.

Board Approval: May 15, 1989.

INSTRUCTION

POL 4.085 COPYRIGHT POLICY

I. Purpose
It is the intent of the Kirtland Community College board of trustees to adhere to the provisions of copyright law.

II. Personnel affected
This policy applies to all personnel employed by Kirtland Community College.

III. Definition of Section 107 of Copyright Law of 1978, "Fair use for Educators"
A new copyright law took effect in January 1978. Section 107 allows educators "fair use" based upon four factors:

1. Purpose and character of use (instructional)
2. Nature of the work (various formats)
3. Amount of work used (usually 10 percent limit)
4. Effect on potential market (sales)

Assuming the use is for classroom instruction, the next criterion applied is "nature of the work". The guidelines below explain what is permissible for each format. The amount of the work legally available under "fair use" varies with the format. Generally, copying should not exceed 10 percent of the total work nor excerpt the creative essence of the work.

IV. Duplication or copying various formats
In order to comply with the copyright law the following provisions shall apply in duplication or copying copyrighted materials in various formats.
  A. Printed materials (except music)
    1. Permitted
      a. Single copies by or at the request of an individual instructor of:
      •a chapter of a book
      •an article from a magazine or newspaper
      •a short story, short essay or short poem, whether or not from a collective work
      •a chart, graph, diagram, drawing, cartoon or picture from a book, magazine or newspaper
      b. Multiple copies by or at the request of an instructor for classroom use in only one course which does not permit obtaining permission (not to exceed one copy per student in a course).
      •a complete poem if less than 250 words if printed on not more than   two pages
      •an excerpt from a long poem, but not to exceed 250 words
      •a complete article, story or essay of less than 2,500 words
      •an excerpt from a larger printed work not to exceed 10 percent of   the whole or 1,000 words, whichever is less
      •one chart, graph, diagram, cartoon or picture per book or magazine issue

2.   **Prohibited.**

a.   Copying more than one work or two excerpts from a single author during one class term.

b.   Copying more than three works from a collective work or periodical volume during one class term.

c.   Copying more than nine sets of multiple copies for distribution to students in one class term.

d.   Copying used to create or replace or substitute for anthologies, compilations or collective works.

e.   Copying of "consumable works" such as workbooks, standardized tests, answer sheets, etc. (note: these prohibitions do not apply to current new magazine and newspapers).

f.   Charging students beyond the actual cost of photocopying.

g.   Making multiple copies without including notice of copyright.

B.   **Sheet and recorded music**

1.   **Permitted**

a.   Emergency copies for an imminent performance are permitted, provided they are replacing purchased copies and replacement is planned.

b.   Multiple copies (one per pupil) of excerpts not constituting an entire performance unit or more than 10 percent of the total work may be made for academic purposes other than performances.

c.   Purchased sheet music may be edited or simplified provided the character of the work isn't distorted or lyrics added or altered.

d.   A single copy of a recorded performance by students may be retained by Kirtland Community College or the individual instructor for evaluation or rehearsal purposes.

e.   A single copy of recording of copyrighted music owned by Kirtland Community college for constructing exercises of examinations and retained for them.

2.   **Prohibited**

a.   Copying to replace or substitute for anthologies, compilations or collections.

b.   Copying from works intended to be "consumable".

c.   Copying for purpose of performance except as permitted by 1.a. above.

d.   Copying to substitute for purchase of music.

e.   Copying without inclusion of copyright notice on the copy.

C.   **Audiovisual**

1.   **Permitted**

a.   Creating a slide or overhead transparency from multiple sources as long as creation does not exceed 10 percent of photographs in one source (book, magazine, filmstrip, etc.) unless the source forbids photographic reproduction.

b.   Creating a single overhead transparency from a single page of a "consumable" workbook.

c.   Reproducing selected slides from a series if reproduction does not exceed 10 percent of total nor excerpting "the essence".

d.   Excerpting sections of a film for a local videotape (not to be shown over cable) if excerpting does not exceed 10 percent of the total nor "the essence" of the work.

e. Stories of literary excerpts may be narrated on tape and duplicated, as long as similar material is not available for sale.

f. Archival copies of video or audio tapes may be produced; however, only a single copy may be used at any time.

g. Copying of phonograph records to cassette may be done but only if the record is then held as the archive copy.

h. Copying of a video tape to another video tape format so the buildings with the non-compatible formats may have access to the same program. Only one tape may be used at a time.

2. **Prohibited**

a. Duplication of a tape (except as permitted above) unless reproduction rights have been secured.

b. Reproducing commercial "ditto masters", individually or in sets (including multimedia kits) if available for sale separately.

c. Except as permitted above, converting one media format to another (i.e. film to videotape) unless permission is secured.

D. **Computer software**

1. **Permitted**

a. A backup copy (new copies) or adaptations created as an essential step in the utilization of the computer program.

b. A single backup copy made for archival purposes (of a backup copy is not provided by the publisher) to be held in case the working copy is destroyed or no longer functions.

c. New copies of software covered by a site licensing agreement with a software publisher (within the limitations specified in the agreement).

d. Copies of "shareware" software may be made for demonstration and evaluation purposes only. Copies of "shareware" software will be accompanied by a copyright notice and the publishers "shareware" license agreement.

2. **Prohibited**

a. Creation of any new copies of copyrighted programs for any purpose other than the four permitted above.

b. Creation of new copies while using a disk-sharing system.

c. Use of any "code breaker" programs to defeat copy protection mechanisms used by software publishers.

d. Any modification of copyrighted software, including but not limited to decompiling, disassembling or otherwise reverse engineering copyrighted code.

e. Distribution of older versions of software when upgrading to a new version. Unless specifically permitted by the publisher, the earlier version and the upgrade are considered by law to be elements of the same copy of the software.

E.   **Off-air recording**
   1.   **Permitted**
      a.   A broadcast program may be recorded off-air simultaneously with transmission and retained by a non-profit educational institution for 45 calendar days after date of recording. After the 45 day retention period, such recordings must be erased or destroyed immediately.
      b.   Off-air recordings may be used once by individual instructors for relevant classroom activities and once for necessary reinforcement during the first 10 consecutive school days after recording.
      c.   After the first 10 school days, recordings may be used up to the end of the 45 day retention period for instructor evaluation purposes only (i.e. to determine if the program should be purchased for the curriculum).
      d.   Such recordings may be made only at the request of and used by individual instructors. No broadcast program may be recorded more than once by the same instructor.
      e.   Such recordings need not be used in their entirety but may not be altered or edited and must include the copyright notice on the program as recorded.

   2.   **Prohibited**
      a.   Off-air recording in anticipation of teacher request.
      b.   Using the recording for instruction after the 10 day period.
      c.   Holding the recording for weeks or indefinitely because
      •units needing the program concepts aren't taught within the 10 day period
      •an interruption or technical problem delayed its use
      •another teacher wished to use it or any other supposed "legitimate" educational reason

V.   **Responsibility for policy**
   A.   The administration in charge of each site is responsible for establishing practices that will enforce this policy at the site level.
   B.   In no case shall any college employee or student use college equipment for duplication which would circumvent the copyright law.
   C.   Kirtland Community College employees who violate copyright law are liable for their own actions.

Adopted March, 1992

AURARIA LIBRARY POLICIES

SUBJECT Guidelines on Copyright

EFFECTIVE DATE March 1993 | **PAGE NO.** 1 **OF** 9 **PAGES**

FILE UNDER SECTION   **NO.** 12

REVISION DATE   **APPROVED BY**

It is the intent of the Auraria Library to adhere to the provisions of the U. S. Copyright Law. (Title 17, US Code) All Library administrators, librarians, and staff shall comply with the provisions of the law. Copyrighted material shall be treated as the property of the copyright holder, with all rights and limitations specified in the law.

FAIR USE

Section 107 of the law allows educators fair use of copyrighted material, meaning that limited numbers of copies of portions of copyrighted works for classroom, scholarship, or research purposes may be made without infringing on copyright. Auraria Library employees shall adhere to the fair use guidelines established in the regulations for printed materials and off-air video recordings.

Fair use guidelines have not yet (as of 3/1/91) been developed for
computer software; therefore, staff shall adhere to restrictions in regulation 3452.3R on duplication of software.

USE OF COPYRIGHT-PROTECTED MATERIAL

Section 107 of the Copyright Law States "...the fair use of a copyrighted work...for purposes such as criticism, comment, news reporting, teaching (including multiple copies for classroom use), scholarship, or research, is not an infringement of copyright." In determining whether the use made in any particular case is a fair use the factors to be considered shall include...

  1. the purpose and character of the use, including whether such use is of a commercial nature or is for nonprofit educational purposes;

  2. the nature of the copyrighted work;

  3. the amount and substantiality of the portion used in relation to the copyrighted work as a whole; and

  4. the effect of the use upon the potential market for or value of the copyrighted work.

Library employees shall apply these fair use guidelines when considering the use of copyrighted print or video material for instructional, scholarship, or research purposes.

The guidelines in the subparts of this regulation explain what the Library shall consider fair use for printed materials and off-air video recordings.   The guidelines were delineated in congressional committee reports in 1976 and 1981.

On occasion, a special notice is provided with some materials specifically prohibiting reproduction of any kind. However, the fair use guidelines do not apply to these materials. Permission to use any part of such works must be secured in writing from the copyright holder.

Whenever copyrighted works are used in part under fair use guidelines or by permission, or in whole by permission, a notice of who owns the copyright must be included on the copy of the work or in the Library-produced work in which the copyrighted materials appears.

PERMITTED AS FAIR USE

1. Single copies at the request of or initiated by a Library employee...

    a. A chapter of a book
    b. A newspaper or magazine article
    c. A short story, short essay, or short poem, whether or not from a collective work
    d. A chart, graph, diagram, drawing, cartoon, or picture from a book, magazine, or newspaper

2. Multiple copies at the request of a faculty member, consultant, or other person involved in classroom instruction (not to exceed one copy per student)...

    a. A complete poem if less than 250 words
    b. From a longer poem, an excerpt of not more than 250 words
    c. A complete article, story, or essay of less than 500 words
    d. An excerpt from a longer printed work not to exceed 10 percent of the whole or 1,000 words, whichever is less. One chart, graph, diagram, cartoon, or picture per book or magazine issue.

DUPLICATION OF PRINTED MATERIALS

To help ensure compliance with the law, the following notice shall be posted on all duplicating machines in the Library. The supervisor of the department in which the machine is located is responsible for seeing that the notice is posted on each machine in his/her area.

University of Colorado at Denver

*The Copyright Law of the United States (Title 17, US Code)
governs the making of photocopies or other reproductions of
copyrighted materials.The person using this equipment is
liable for any infringement.*

DUPLICATION OF ORIGINAL RESEARCH MATERIALS

It is the researcher's obligation to satisfy copyright
regulations when using original research materials found in
archives and manuscript collections. The Archives & Special
Collections Department will copy unrestricted portions of
collections after a researcher has read and signed a Request for
Duplication form. The Department will also inform a researcher
about known copyrighted material, the owner or owners of the
copyrights when known, and the researcher's obligations with
regard to such material.

PROHIBITED COPYING

1.   Copying more than one work or two excerpts from a
     single author during one class term or per workshop or
     series of training sessions

2.   Copying more than three works from a collective work
     or periodical volume during one class term or per
     workshop or series of training sessions

3.   Copying more than nine instances for distribution to
     students during one class term or in one workshop or
     series of training sessions

4.   Copying used to create or replace or substitute for
     anthologies or collective works

5.   Copying of consumable works such as workbooks,
     standardized tests, answer sheets, etc..

Note: These prohibitions do not apply to current news magazines
or   newspapers.

OFF-THE-AIR VIDEO RECORDING

To help ensure compliance with the law, the following notice
shall be posted on all video tape recorders in use in the
Library. The supervisor of the department in which the machine
is located is responsible for seeing that the notice is posted
on each machine in his/her area.

> **Warning:** Federal Law provides severe civil and criminal
> penalties for the unauthorized reproduction, distribution
> or exhibition of copyrighted motion pictures, video tapes
> or video discs.

The following guidelines have been developed to apply only to
off-air recording by nonprofit educational institutions:

University of Colorado at Denver

PERMITTED AS FAIR USE

1. A broadcast program may be recorded off-air simultaneously with broadcast transmission (including simultaneous cable retransmission) and retained by a nonprofit educational institution for a period not to exceed the first 45 consecutive calendar days after the date of recording. Upon conclusion of such retention period, all off-air recordings must be erased or destroyed immediately. Broadcast programs are television programs transmitted by television stations for reception by the general public without charge.

2. An off-air recording may be used once by individual teachers, consultants, or other trainers in the course of relevant instructional or training activities, and repeated once only when instructional reinforcement is necessary in classrooms or similar settings, during the first 10 consecutive work days in the 45-calendar-day retention period.

3. Off-air recordings may be made only at the request of and used by individual teachers, consultants, or other trainers, and may not be regularly recorded in anticipation of requests. No broadcast program may be recorded off-air more than once at the request of the same teacher, consultant, or other trainer, regardless of the number of times the program may be broadcast.

4. A limited number of copies may be reproduced from each off-air recording to meet the legitimate needs of teachers and other trainers under these guidelines. Each such additional copy shall be subject to all provisions governing the original recording.

5. After the first 10 consecutive work days, off-air recordings may be used up to the end of the 45-calendar-day retention period only for evaluation purposes (i.e., to determine whether or not to include the broadcast program as part of ongoing training activities--in which case permission from the producer would be required.)

6. Off-air recordings need not be used in their entirety, but the recorded programs may not be altered from their original content.

PROHIBITED USE

1. Off-air recording in anticipation of teacher or other staff member requests

2. Using the recording for instruction after the 10 day use period

3. Holding the recording for weeks or indefinitely because...

    •   units, workshops, or training sessions requiring the program concepts were not held within the 10-day use period

    •   an interruption or technical problem delayed its use

    •   another teacher, consultant, or trainer wishes to use it

    •   of any assumed "legitimate" educational reason.

4. Physically or electronically merging or combining off-air recordings to constitute instructional anthologies or compilations.

5. Using off-air recordings or programs rented or purchased from a video store for entertainment during the work day or evenings (This constitutes a public showing for which special fees must be paid.)

6. Using Library-owned equipment for making or playing back copies that are not legally acquired.

USE OF PROPRIETARY SOFTWARE PRODUCTS

It is the intent of the Auraria Library to adhere to the provisions of copyright law (Title 17, US Code) and publishers license agreements, including trade secret provisions, in the area of proprietary software products. (Proprietary products are those made or marketed by persons having exclusive manufacturing and sales rights, who may or may not be the copyright holders.)
Therefore, persons may use or cause to be used on office computing equipment only software that is included in one of the following categories.

a. Public domain (i.e., uncopyrighted) software
b. Software covered by a licensing agreement with the software author, authors, vendor, or developer, whichever is applicable (a licensing agreement is a legal contract authorizing use)
c. Software purchased by the Library, with a record of the purchase on file
d. Software purchased by the user, with a record of purchase available for Library verification
e. Software donated to the Library and officially accepted as property of the Auraria Library
f. Software being reviewed by staff or demonstrated by vendors in order to reach a decision about possible future purchase, license, or acceptance of a donation

g.   Software written or developed by the Library in general or an employee who gives the Library permission to copy

h.   Software developed by a nonemployee under contract to the Library for use by the Library or to assist in training Library personnel

In addition, none of the software in the categories listed above may be used or obtained in violation of copyright law or licensing agreements or other limitations set by the Library.

Licensing agreements or other forms of documentation covering software shall be kept on file at the Library Automated Services Office. (See below for information on submitting a Request for Contract, the form used to obtain approval for a licensing agreement.)

USE OF PURCHASED SOFTWARE PRODUCTS

The guidelines set forth below shall be followed in the handling of all software purchased for use by the Library.

1.   On receipt of software and prior to use, check the package and any accompanying documentation or materials. Look carefully for:

>   warnings
>   references to copying restrictions
>   license agreements
>   special seals or wrappings
>   trade secret references

2.   If a license agreement or other contractual agreement is part of the software package, carefully read the conditions of the agreement and look closely for any limitations on copying, use on specific computers, or other aspects of use. If the wording is difficult to interpret, immediately contact the Auraria Library Systems Librarian for assistance.

3.   If the terms are not acceptable, consult the Systems Librarian for possible courses of action:

>   the software and documentation may be returned for a refund;

>   the company may be contacted to see if a more acceptable agreement can be negotiated; or

>   the Auraria Library administration may be consulted to determine other options.

When a decision is made to negotiate a new agreement, forward the changed agreement and all documentation of the company's approval of the changes to the Systems Coordinator for processing.

University of Colorado at Denver

4. If the terms of the agreement are acceptable, proceed with installation and use of the software according the agreement. Complete the agreement form and forward it to the Systems Librarian. All contracts, license agreements, or other legal agreements with outside organizations must be reviewed and signed by the appropriate administrator of the Auraria Library.

DUPLICATION OF SOFTWARE

No person shall copy or cause to be copied on Library computing equipment any copyrighted or proprietary programs, except for archival purposes as explained below. Proprietary programs are those to which someone, who may or may not be the copyright holder, has exclusive rights, including trade secret protection.

To help insure compliance with the prohibitions on duplication of
software, the following notice shall be affixed to each computer in use in the Library. The supervisor of the department in which the machine is located is responsible for seeing that the notice is posted on each machine in his/her area.

Illegal copies of copyrighted programs may not be made or used on computers or computer systems belonging to the Auraria Library.

One archival, or backup, copy of copyrighted software purchased by or donated to the Library may be made, unless an applicable licensing agreement prohibits copying for any purpose. An adaptation of a copyrighted computer program may be made only if it is for archival purposes and is essential to using the program on a particular computer, and does not violate terms of a license agreement. Archival copies shall be destroyed should use of the computer programs cease to be rightful. All site licensing and local area network licensing shall be complied with.

No Library employee shall make copies of copyrighted software documentation without written permission from the copyright owner (permission archival copy may be given to the documentation itself) or as permitted under the doctrine of "fair use".

MATERIALS COPYRIGHTED BY THE Library

Materials developed by staff within the scope or as a result of employment by the Library are eligible for copyright. These materials include, but are not limited to, books, directories, periodicals, musical compositions, works of art, photographs, prints and pictorial illustrations, motion pictures, slides, video and audio tapes, computer software, and films.

Publication is defined as "the distribution of copies of a work to the public by sale or other transfer of ownership, or by rental, lease, or lending."

A notice of copyright shall be affixed to all materials to be copyrighted by the Library, commencing with first publication. The act of publishing a work with the copyright notice affixed secures the copyright protection. (see below for example)

Copyright 1992 Auraria Library or Copyright 1992 John Jones, Auraria Library

When the finished version of copyrightable materials has been prepared, formal approval to copyright shall be obtained from the appropriate Library administrator.

The Director/Dean of the Auraria Library may appoint an ad hoc committee to review and make recommendations on proposed copyrighting of specific materials by the Library.

All materials copyrighted by the Library shall be original, unless the required clearances and permissions have been obtained in writing from the copyright holders.

Publications prepared by the Auraria Library incorporating works which are not original may still be copyrighted by the Library to protect the original portions therein.

If materials are produced under a university grant, copyrights shall be secured according to the copyright guidelines published by the University of Colorado at Denver. Authors shall consult the appropriate funding agency office regarding procedures to be followed when considering copyright of materials produced under the auspices of direct grants or contracts.

Original material may be registered by the Copyright Office of the Library of Congress at the discretion of the University of Colorado at Denver.

APPENDIX A

117.   Limitations on exclusive rights: Computer programs.

Notwithstanding the provisions of section 106, it is not an infringement of the owner of a copy of a computer program to make or authorize the making of another copy or adaptation of that computer program provided:

(1)   that such copy or adaptation is created as an essential step in the utilization of the computer program in conjunction with a machine and that it is used in no other manner or,

(2)   that such new copy or adaptation is for archival purposes only and that all archival copies are destroyed in the event that continued possession of the computer program should cease to be rightful.

Any exact copies prepared in accordance with the provisions of this section may be leased, sold, or otherwise transferred, along with the copy from which such copies were prepared, only as part of the lease, sale or other transfer of all rights in the program. Adaptations so prepared may be transferred only with the authorization of the copyright owner.

INFORMATIONAL DOCUMENTS

Pikes Peak Community College
Broome Community College
Tallahassee Community College
Pima County Community College
Chattanooga State Technical Community College
Manatee Community College

PikesPeak Community College

Learning Resource Center

A GUIDE TO WHAT'S LEGAL
AND WHAT'S NOT

Pikes Peak Community College

My special thanks to Bob Armintor, LRC Staff Member, for his excellent work in compiling all the information in this booklet. Copyright issues arise almost daily when dealing with the dissemination of information, no matter what format. Bob agreed to take the "bull by the horns" and research this topic.

Ivan Bender (Appendix A) gives a good introduction to copyright. I encourage everyone to take the time to read it and this whole document. Bob has done a very good job in formatting this document for easy and quick reading. Doing so will give you a better understanding of the types of copyright issues we face while trying to provide a service to our patrons.

Thanks again, Bob!

Camila A. Alire, Ed. D.
Director
Learning Resources Center
Pikes Peak Community College

CAA/glc

ii

-TABLE OF CONTENTS-

-APPENDICIES-

INTRODUCTION

The Copyright Maze!   For most educators that title is most apt.   Trying to find one's way through the sometimes complicated rules governing the use of copyrighted materials can cause one to wonder if it's all worth it!

This guide is designed to help the faculty and staff here at PPCC to know what the law is with regard to print and non-print materials, and to answer some of the basic questions most often asked.   It is not designed to reassure those who would like to circumvent the law as it is now written.   P.L. 94-553 is the law of the land, and we, as educators and citizens, must follow its provisions no matter how illogical they may seem.   If this law or its interpretations are repressive to quality education, then we should lobby to change it.   However, we are obligated to uphold the law to the best of our ability, regardless of what has been done in the past.

There's quite a bit of information in this guide.   You may not want or have time to read it all at one sitting.   So, just pick out those sections that are of immediate interest to you and review them.   But, at some time, please read all of the guide from cover to cover.   I think that you will find it helpful. And, ignorance of the law is no defense in the event you are sued!

I would like to thank Eric Feder, Director of Media Services for Poudre School District R-1 in Fort Collins, for granting permission for me to adapt and edit their copyright guidelines manual.   Most of the material contained herein was gleaned from that source.   Also my thanks to Ivan R. Bender, copyright attorney for the Television Licensing Center in Chicago, IL for permission to reprint a number of columns which have appeared in their newsletter.   And, I thank Art Boisselle, Johnny Kloefkorn, and Sol Zlochower of PPCC for permitting me to interview them with regard to the copyright issue (see Appendices I-K).

If you have additional questions concerning copyright, please do not hesitate to contact me (x537) and I will be happy to research an answer for you.   I do not claim to be an expert on the law, and Title 17 of the United States Code Annotated is a fairly thick volume, so it may take some time!

Bob Armintor
Media Specialist
Learning Resources Center
Pikes Peak Community College
Production & Distribution Services
(A-204)

RPA/glc

Pikes Peak Community College

1

–WHAT IS "FAIR-USE" OF COPYRIGHTED MATERIALS?–

"Fair-use" allows instructors, media specialist, students, and others working in a nonprofit educational institution to duplicate work without permission from or payment to copyright owners. In order to do so, four "fair-use" key criteria must be met. they are:

1) Purpose and character of the use, including whether such use is of a commercial nature or is for nonprofit educational purposes---in other words, how will the materials be used and by whom?

2) Nature of the copyrighted work---what is the format of the work? Print? Television programming? Music? Software? etc. Each format has different allowable uses before permission from the copyright holder is required.

3) Amount and substantiality of the portion used in relation to the copyrighted work as a whole---in other words, how much of the work will be used? How important is the section? Permission from the copyright holder may have to be requested depending upon the answers.

4) Effect of the use upon the potential market for or value of the copyrighted work. Will the intended use cause the copyright holder to lose sales?

–RIGHTS OF THE COPYRIGHT HOLDER–

The rights protected by copyright are as follows:

a) Reproduction of the work in any form.

b) Distribution of copies; only the copyright holder may sell, lease, or give away copies.

c) Adaptation into a new form, including new musical arrangements.

d) Performance of the work to include musical presentations, pantomines, movies, audiovisual formats, pictures and graphs, recitations, dances, plays, and television and radio broadcasts.

In 1976 Congress passed the revised Copyright Law (P.L. 94-553). This law went into effect on January 1, 1978, and was designed to take into account the newer technologies developed since the enactment of the previous law in 1909.

The new copyright law sets the term of copyright to the life of the author plus 50 years, 75 years for corporate or anonymous works, and the life of the last living author plus 50 years for multi-author works. All works still protected by the 1909 law, when the new law went into effect in January 1978, were given 75 year extensions.

Pikes Peak Community College

-"FAIR-USE" GUIDELINES FOR BOOKS AND PERIODICALS-

1) Single Copying

A single copy may be made of any of the following by or for an instructor at his/her individual request for his/her scholarly research or use in teaching or in preparation to teach a course:

a) A chapter from a book
b) An article from a periodical or newspaper
c) A short story, short essay, or short poem, whether or not from a collected work
d) A chart, graph, diagram, drawing, cartoon, or picture from a book, periodical, or newspaper

2) Multiple Copies for Classroom Use

Multiple copies (not to exceed one copy per pupil in a course) may be made by or for an instructor for classroom use or discussion, provided that:

a) The copying meets the tests for brevity and spontaneity as defined below, and
b) Meets the cumulative effect test as defined below, and
c) Each copy includes a notice of copyright

Definitions

Brevity (see Appendix B)

1) Poetry

a) A complete poem if less than 250 words and if printed on not more than two pages, or
b) From a longer poem, an excerpt of not more than 250 words.

2) Prose

a) Either a complete article, story, essay of less than 2500 words, or
b) An excerpt of not more than 1000 words or 10% of the work, from any prose work, but in any event, a minimum of 500 words.

(Each numerical limit stated above may be expanded to permit the completion of an unfinished line of a poem or an unfinished prose paragraph.

c) Illustrations: one chart, graph, diagram, drawing, cartoon, or picture per book or per periodical issue
d) "Special" works: Certain works in poetry, prose, or in "poetic prose" which often combine language with illustrations and which are intended sometimes for children and at other times for a more general audience fall short of 2500 words in their entirety. Paragraph "b" above notwithstanding, such "special works" may not be reproduced in their entirety; however, an excerpt comprising not more than two of the published pages of such special works and containing not more than 10% of the words found in the text thereof, may be reproduced.

Spontaneity

- a) The copying is at the instance and inspiration of the individual instructor, and
- b) The inspiration and decision to use the work and the moment of its use for maximum teaching effectiveness are so close in time that it would be unreasonable to expect a timely reply to a request for permission.

Cumulative Effect

- a) The copying of the material is for only one course in which it will be used.
- b) Not more than one short poem, article, story, essay, or two excerpts may be copied from the same author, nor more than three from the same collective work or periodical volume during the semester.
- c) There shall not be more than nine instances of such multiple copying for one course during a semester.

(The limitations stated in "b" and "c" above shall not apply to current news periodicals and newspapers and current news sections of other periodicals.)

3) Prohibitions as to 1) and 2) above

The following should be prohibited, not withstanding any of the above:

- a) Copying shall not be used to create or to replace or substitute for anthologies, compilations, or collective works. Such replacement or substitution may occur whether copies of various works or excerpts therefrom are accumulated or reproduced and used separately.
- b) There shall be no copying of or from works intended to be "consumable" in the course of study or teaching. These items include workbooks, exercises, standardized tests, test booklets and answer sheets, and like consumable material.
- c) Copying shall not:

  1) Substitute for the purchase of books, publishers' reports, or periodicals.
  2) Be directed by higher authority.
  3) Be repeated with respect to the same item by the same instructor from semester to semester.

- d) No charge shall be made to the student beyond the actual cost of photocopying.

-COMMON QUESTIONS RELATING TO "FAIR-USE"
OF MATERIALS CONTAINED IN BOOKS AND PERIODICALS-

a)   I am teaching a class and would like to make a copy of Chapter 2 for each student. May I?

NO. The guidelines suggest that the chapter cannot be copied unless it consists of less than 1,000 words or 10% of the book, whichever is less. You may, however, make a copy of Chapter 2 for your own research.

b)   Instructor "A." has a copy of a five-page book which was published in Great Britain. She makes five additional copies of the book to use once every year with a particular course. She asks, "Do I really have to send to Great Britain for those additional copies?"

YES. We observe the copyright laws of other countries and they observe ours.

c)   A division secretary is directed by an instructor to make 75 copies of a commercially produced workbook. Technically who is responsible for this violation?

BOTH the secretary and the instructor, the instructor for asking and the secretary for doing.

d)   May I make ten copies of the title page of a library book?

YES. You may make one copy per student of any excerpt which is less than 1,000 words or less than 10% of the book, whichever is less.

e)   May I make copies of a commercially produced worksheet?

NO. There shall be no copying of or from works intended to be consumable in the course of study or teaching.

f)   May I make 20 copies of a Newsweek article to distribute to my class?

YES. You may as long as it is less than 2,500 words (test of brevity), and it would be unreasonable to expect a response in time if a letter seeking permission to copy were written (test of spontaneity). However, you may not use these copies semester after semester without written permission.

g)   May I charge students for materials copied for use in class?

YES, but the cost may not exceed the actual cost of photocopying.

h)   May I made a transparency of a worksheet to help my students work through a particular concept?

YES. But only one copy may be made.

i)   Must I include the notice of copyright from the original work on all copies I make?

YES.

Pikes Peak Community College

-"FAIR-USE" GUIDELINES FOR COMPUTER SOFTWARE-

In 1980, by Public Law 95-517, Section 117 of P.L. 94-553 was amended to
address the issue of duplication of computer software. A "computer program"
was defined as a "set of statements or instructions to be used directly in a
computer in order to bring about a certain result."

The law permits the <u>owner</u>, not leasor, of a copy of a computer program to make
<u>another copy</u> or adaptation of that program if the following criteria are met:

1) The new copy or adaptation is created in order to be able to use the
    program in conjunction with the equipment and it is used in no other
    manner.

2) The new copy of adaptation is for <u>archival purposes only</u>, <u>not for use as
    an additional copy</u>. And, that all archival copies are to be destroyed in
    the event that continued possession of the computer program should cease
    to be rightful.

3) Any copies prepared or adapted may not be leased, sold, or otherwise
    transferred without the authorization of the <u>copyright owner</u>.

Prohibitions

The creation of any new copies of copyrighted programs for any purpose other
than in sections 1 and 2 above, such as:

a) Multiple booting

b) Putting a program on a hard disk for networking purposes

c) Downloading a program to a terminal and then saving the program on a disk,
    tape, or other such storage device.

—COMMON QUESTIONS RELATING TO "FAIR-USE" OF COMPUTER SOFTWARE-

a) May a disk which a company designates and sells as a "back-up" copy be used as a work disk?

NO. "Back-up" or "archival" copies are to be used <u>only</u> in the event the original or work disk is destroyed and then only until a new copy can be acquired from the publisher/distributor. Further, all archival copies are to be destroyed and/or returned in the event that the continued possession of the computer program is no longer rightful (i.e.-lease expires).

b) May I make a "back-up" copy of any program I buy if the publisher does not provide one?

YES. However, it may not be used unless the original is destroyed and then only until a new copy can be acquired from the copyright holder.

c) May I make a "back-up" copy of any program I <u>lease?</u>

NO. You may make a "back-up" copy of programs you <u>purchase</u> only.

d) Must there be written permission from a software company to multiple boot a disk when this procedure is not specifically mentioned in the program documentation?

YES. Multiple booting involves making a copy, although temporary, in the computer's memory.

e) Can we use "Locksmith" or other similar programs and systems to make a copy of a program we <u>own?</u>

YES. A copy may be made, but only as a "back-up" (see "b" above).

-"FAIR-USE" GUIDELINES FOR SHEET AND RECORDED MUSIC-

Representatives of the Music Publisher's Association of the U.S., Inc., the National Music Publishers' Assoc., Inc., the Music Teachers' National Assoc., the Music Educators' National Conference, the National Association of Schools of Music, and the Ad Hoc Committee on Copyright Law Revision, developed the following guidelines for "fair-use" of sheet and recorded music.

1) Permissible Uses

a) Emergency copying to replace purchased copies which for any reason are not available for an imminent performance provided purchased replacements shall be substituted in due course.

b) For academic purposes, other than performance, single or multiple copies or excerpts of works may be made, provided that the excerpts do not comprise a part of the whole which would constitute a performable unit such as a section, movement or aria, but in no case more than 10% of the whole work. The number of copies shall not exceed one copy per student.

c) Printed copies which have been purchased may be edited or simplified provided that the fundamental character of the work is not distorted or the lyrics, if any, altered or lyrics added, if none exist.

d) A single copy of recordings of performances by students may be made for evaluation or rehearsal purposes and may be retained by the educational institution or individual instructor.

e) A single copy of a sound recording (such as a tape, disc, or cassette) of copyrighted music may be made from sound recordings owned by an educational institution or an individual instructor for the purpose of constructing aural exercises or examinations and may be retained by the educational institution or individual instructor.
(This pertains only to the copyright of the music itself and not to any copyright which may exist in the sound recordings.)

2) Prohibitions

a) Copying to create, replace, or substitute for anthologies, compilations, or collected works.

b) Copying of or from works intended to be consumable in the course of study or of teaching such as workbooks, exercises, standardized tests, answer sheets, and like material.

c) Copying for the purpose of performance, except as in section 1 "a" above.

d) Copying for the purpose of substituting for the purchase of music, except as in section 1 "a" and "b" above.

e) Copying without inclusion of the copyright notice which appears on the printed copy.

COMMON QUESTIONS RELATING TO "FAIR-USE" OF
SHEET AND RECORDED MUSIC-

a) Do publishers usually grant permission for use of their materials by educational institutions?

   YES.

b) May I have my class write and perform parodies of popular songs?

   YES. An idea or theme is not protectable. It is the manner of expression that is. It is one thing to alter the lyrics of a song, still using the original expression, and quite another to do a true parody. The latter is permissible while the former is not. The same applies to prose and poetry.

c) May I make a copy of a portion of a record so a student can better learn his/her part?

   YES. The excerpts must not comprise a part of the whole which would constitute a performable unit such as a section, movement, or aria, but in no case shall exceed 10% for the whole work.

d) May I make a video or audio recording of a student performance of a copyrighted work?

   YES, provided it is for evaluation or rehearsal purposes only. It may be retained by the educational institution or the instructor.

e) May I audio tape several segments of phonorecords and audio cassettes to instruct or test my students?

   NO. You may not create anthologies.

f) Must I include the copyright notice on every copy I make?

   YES.

g) Is the music broadcast by radio stations covered by copyright?

   YES. Copying and duplicating of said music is an infringement of the copyright law.

-"FAIR-USE" GUIDELINES FOR OFF-AIR RECORDING OF BROADCAST PROGRAMMING FOR EDUCATIONAL PURPOSES-

1. The guidelines were developed to apply only to off-air recording by non-profit educational institutions.

2. A broadcast program may be recorded off-air simultaneously with broadcast transmission (including simultaneous cable retransmission) and retained by a nonprofit educational institution for a period not to exceed the first forty-five (45) consecutive calendar days after date of recording. Upon conclusion of such retention period, all off-air recordings must be erased or destroyed immediately. "Broadcast programs" are television programs transmitted by television stations for reception by the general public without charge.

3. Off-air recordings may be used once by individual teachers in the course of relevant teaching activities, and repeated once only when instructional reinforcement is necessary, in classrooms and similar places devoted to instruction within a single building, cluster or campus, as well as in the homes of students receiving formalized home instruction, during the first ten (10) consecutive school days in the forty-five (45) calendar day retention period. "School days" are school session days--not counting weekends, holidays, vacations, examination periods, or other scheduled interruptions--within the forty-five (45) calendar day retention period.

4. Off-air recordings may be made only at the request of and used by individual teachers, and may not be regularly recorded in anticipation of requests. No broadcast program may be recorded off-air more than once at the request of the same teacher, regardless of the number of times the program may be broadcast.

5. A limited number of copies may be reproduced from each off-air recording to meet the legitimate needs of teachers under these guidelines. Each such additional copy shall be subject to all provisions governing the original recording.

6. After the first ten (10) consecutive school days, off-air recordings may be used up to the end of the forty-five calendar day retention period only for teacher evaluation purposes, i.e., to determine whether or not to include the broadcast program in the teaching curriculum, and may not be used in the recording institution for student exhibition or any other non-evaluation purpose without authorization.

7. Off-air recordings need not be used in their entirety, but the recorded programs may not be altered from their original content. Off-air recordings may not be physically or electronically combined or merged to constitute teaching anthologies or compilations.

8. All copies of off-air recordings must include the copyright notice on the broadcast program as recorded.

9. Educational institutions are expected to establish appropriate control procedures to maintain the integrity of these guidelines.

(For more information see Appendix C.)

-EDUCATIONAL USE OF PRERECORDED VIDEOTAPES LABELED "FOR HOME USE ONLY"-

Videotapes so marked may be used in an educational institution <u>if</u>:

1) It is used in the course of face-to-face teaching activities.

2) The copy used has not been illegally made or brought into the classroom in violation of the P.L. 94-553.

3) The display or transmission of the program:

   a) Is a regular part of the systematic instructional activities of a nonprofit educational institution, <u>and</u>
   b) Is directly related and of material assistance to the teaching content of the transmission, <u>and</u>
   c) Is made primarily for reception in classrooms or similar places normally devoted to instruction. . .

(For more information see Appendix D & E.)

-"FAIR-USE" GUIDELINES FOR THE USE OF TELEVISION PROGRAMMING
RECEIVED VIA A SATELLITE DISH-

According to Federal Communications law, satellite transmissions are private communications and cannot be viewed or recorded by others in a business/institutional setting. They can be viewed and taped by individuals in their home as long as scrambled signals are not unscrambled without authorization. Tapes made in this manner <u>cannot</u> be brought into the classroom.

All recording done by an educational institution must have prior authorization. U.S. Government programming, such as NASA transmissions during space missions, are an exception to this rule and are allowed.

(For further information see Appendix F.)

—COMMON QUESTIONS RELATING TO "FAIR-USE" OF TELEVISION PROGRAMMING—

a) May I videotape a program off the local cable system?

YES. You may record it provided it is on the basic service and is not a premium (pay) channel. You may retain the copy for only 45 calendar days. It may be used in direct instruction only one(1) time per class with an additional time for follow up within the first ten (10) class days only. The program may not be edited in any way. (See also Appendix D.)

b) May this videotaped program be used year after year?

NO. It must be erased after 45 days. And, an instructor may request that an individual program be taped only once regardless of the number of times it airs.

c) If more than one instructor wants to preview this program, may I make copies?

YES. All copies are subject to the provisions governing the original recording.

d) The Supreme Court said I can videotape anything in my home and keep it forever. May I bring these tapes into my class for use?

They must meet the criteria in "a" above.

e) May I rent a videotape or bring to class a tape I have purchased which is labeled "for home use only?"

YES. Section 110 (1) provides that videotapes so labeled may be used if they are part of "face-to-face" instructional activities. The use must be part of the instructional program and cannot be shown for recreation or entertainment.

f) What are some examples of activities this would prohibit?

--The showing of a videotape as a reward or at holiday times just for entertainment.

g) Does the copyright law distinguish between televising via the closed circuit system to the classroom(s) and using a VCR in the individual classroom(s)?

NO. The use must comply with all provisions of the copyright law and the guidelines for use.

h) Do the same guidelines for recording and playback apply to broadcast or open-air television programming?

YES. Retention periods and face-to-face instructional contact all apply.

i) If a program was taped just before a break or vacation period, can it be kept and used when classes resume?

YES. Provided that the 45 day retention period is adhered to. You may not tape a program in May and then show it in September.

Pikes Peak Community College

j) May I record something off my home satellite dish and bring it to the college for use in my class?

NO. Satellite transmissions cannot be used in educational settings without permission.

k) May I tape or have the Learning Resources Center staff tape a satellite transmission for preview by the instructional staff to determine whether or not to participate in a proposed telecourse?

YES. However, it must not be used in an instructional manner without permission of the copyright holder. And, the 45 day retention/preview period must be followed.

l) If a copyright holder does not wish to sell or rent a particular program, may I use it beyond the "fair-use" period?

NO. The copyright holder has the exclusive right to do what he/she wishes with his/her programming. This includes not distributing it! However, I think you will find that most producers/distributors wish to sell their products to the widest audience possible.

-"FAIR-USE" GUIDELINES FOR OTHER MEDIA-

Although the new law does not specifically address itself, at this time, to published/distributed items other than print, music, computer software, and television, it is safe to assume that audiovisual materials such as slides, filmstrips, filmloops, 16mm films, cassettes, etc. are protected to the same extent and in like manner.

For these kinds of items, instructors should apply the "fair-use" criteria and/or definitions of brevity, spontaneity, and cumulative effect for each intended use. Both faculty and staff are encouraged to seek permission (written or verbal) from the copyright holder whenever possible.

—COMMON QUESTIONS RELATED TO "FAIR-USE" OF OTHER MEDIA—

a) May I made a copy of an audio or videocassette when two instructors need to use it at the same time?

   NO. Only the copyright holder has the right to authorize the making and distribution of copies.

b) May I make an audiocassette copy of a phonodisc so that it will be more convenient to use?

   NO. Only the copyright holder can authorize a change of format.

Your Right To Copy:

A Handbook

Broome Community College

Fall 1993

Broome Community College

YOUR RIGHT TO COPY

A Handbook for College Personnel

Introduction

This handbook of information, guidelines and procedures has been compiled as a reference guide for College faculty, staff and administrators to help answer everyday questions about the use and reproduction of copyrighted materials and to provide information about College procedure as it applies to the photocopying and reproduction of copyrighted materials in various formats. It offers guidance about what copying is permissible and appropriate in the context of higher education in general and in the context of Broome Community College in particular. It should not be used as a substitute for sound legal advice. Questions which go beyond the scope of the information in this handbook should be referred to SUNY counsel through the Campus Copyright Officer (Director of the Learning Resource Center). There is also the Copyright Hotline, a service of the Association for Information Media and Equipment which may be of some assistance. (1-800-444-4203)

Much of the text of this handbook is taken with permission from the Copyright Handbook of Hudson Valley Community College and from copyright legislation and legislative guidelines. Some of the text has been adapted from policies and guidelines such as: the Association of Research Libraries' *Briefing Paper on Copyright* and the American Library Association's *Model Policy Concerning College and University Photocopying.* These documents address copyright issues of interest to institutions of higher education and present a clear and balanced approach to a complex topic.

We are grateful to SUNY-Albany and Hudson Valley Community College for granting permission to modify their Copyright handbooks for adoption as the official Broome Community College Copyright Handbook.

BCC Copyright Officer: *Director of Learning Resource Center*

Retention of licenses and permissions, if acquired through college contracts, is in the Purchasing Office. Otherwise, the individual requestor will hold the master. Departments may wish to coordinate such activity.

The Purpose of Copyright

The primary purpose of the copyright law of the United States is to foster the creation and dissemination of intellectual works for the public welfare. Copyright is a constitutionally conceived property right which is designed to promote the progress of science and the useful arts by securing for an author the benefits of his or her original work of authorship for a limited time (U.S. Constitution, Art. 1, Sec. 8). The copyright law attempts to balance the rights of copyright owners with those of users. In order to encourage the production of creative works, the copyright law provides incentive for the creators by granting them exclusive rights to reproduce and distribute their work. These exclusive rights of the copyright holder are, however, subject to important exceptions. **Certain public and private uses of copyrighted works are allowed under the law without the copyright holder's permission if they can be determined to be fair use.** Information about what constitutes fair use is discussed in detail in this handbook and should be read with care.

Copyright Requirements

The Copyright Act of 1976 (hereafter referred to as the **Copyright Act**) defines the types of works protected by copyright and specifies the requirements for copyright protection. Works must be of original authorship representing an appreciable amount of creativity and fixed in a tangible medium of expression. Protection begins from the moment a work is committed to writing, recorded on audio cassette tape, or filmed. Works of authorship include the following categories: (1) literary works; (2) musical works; (3) dramatic works; (4) pantomimes and choreographic works; (5) pictorial, graphic and sculptural works; (6) motion pictures and other audiovisual works; (7) sound recordings.

Copyright Notice

A work is protected by copyright from the moment it is fixed in tangible form on paper, tape, film, etc. When a work is published, it must be published with proper copyright notice or, under certain circumstances, the copyright may be forfeited. Proper copyright notice usually consists of the following three elements:

  A. The symbol © or the word "Copyright," or the abbreviation "Copr."; or, in the case of phonorecord, the symbol P;

  B. The year of first publication of the work;

  C. The name of the copyright owner.

Of the three options listed in A, it is recommended that the symbol © be used, since that is the form of notice agreed on by all the countries who are signatories to the Universal Copyright Convention.

For books, copyright notices are usually found on the back of the title page. Notices on periodicals are either on the title page, the first page of text, or in the masthead. Works published prior to January 1, 1978, were required to contain a copyright notice to be protected by copyright law.

Under the present Copyright Act, notice requirements have been relaxed so that an absence of notice on works published after January 1, 1978, when the Act became law, does not necessarily mean that the work is in the public domain. However, omission of the notice does mean that an innocent infringer is not liable for damages. If, after normal inspection, a person copies and distributes a work on which no copyright notice is visible and the copyright holder finds out about it and claims infringement of copyright, the copyright holder could prevent the further distribution of copies but could not hold the person liable for damages. Following fair use practices should prevent infringement of copyright, innocent or otherwise.

Sometimes the words "All Rights Reserved" are printed underneath a copyright notice. Sometimes statements are added such as: "No part of this publication may be reproduced or transmitted in any form or by any means, electronic or mechanical [etc., etc.]." These statements are used to intimidate or mislead people and prevent photocopying and duplication. They are largely meaningless statements and do not override the concept of fair use rights as discussed in this handbook.

Duration of Copyright

Under the new law, copyright protection is in effect for the life of the author plus 50 years. For works with multiple authors, it is the death of the last surviving author that triggers the beginning of the fifty years. Works made for hire, works written anonymously, and works written under a pseudonym are protected for 75 years after the date of the first publication or 100 years after date of creation, whichever expires first.

This is a significant extension of the pre-1978 term of copyright protection which lasted 28 years from the date of first publication, with an option to renew for one additional 47-year term. Determining the copyright status of a work is no longer as simple as it once was and faculty and staff who have questions about copyright duration should rely on the services of the U.S. Copyright Office (LM 455, Library of Congress, Washington, D.C. 20559 - [202] 287-9100), which investigates the copyright status of a work on an hourly fee basis.

In general, we can say that all copyrights prior to 1918 have expired. Copyrights granted after 1918 may have been renewed; however, the work will probably not contain notice of the renewal. Therefore, it should be assumed all writings dated 1918 or later are covered by a valid copyright, unless information to the contrary is obtained from the owner of the copyright or the U.S. Copyright Office.

Works Not Protected by Copyright

Anyone may reproduce, without restriction, works which were never copyrighted.

Writings published prior to January 1, 1978 without copyright notices are not protected and may be reproduced without restriction.

Please keep in mind that copyright notice requirements have been relaxed since 1978, so that the absence of notice on works published after January 1, 1978 does not necessarily mean the work is in the public domain. To avoid questions of copyright infringement, faculty and staff wishing to copy these materials should follow fair use practices.

Anyone may reproduce, without constraint, published works whose copyrights have expired.

All copyrights dated earlier than 1918 have expired. Copyrights dated 1918 or later may have expired. We recommend that faculty and staff should either assume that copyright protection is still in effect for these materials or inquire whether protection is still in effect. Inquiries can be made to the U.S. Copyright Office in Washington, D.C.

Anyone may reproduce, without permission, a publication of the U.S. Government.

U.S. Government publications may be copied freely because they are not copyrightable. They are considered as being within the public domain. This category consists of documents prepared by an officer or employee of the U.S. Government as part of the person's official duties. It does not extend to documents published by others with the support of government grants and contracts. These works may or may not be protected by copyright, depending on the specifics of the contract under which they were created. Although their copyright status may not be readily apparent, it may be reasonable to assume that much of this material is protected by copyright.

A privately published work which consists preponderantly of one or more works of the U.S. Government must include in the notice of copyright a statement identifying the portions of the work protected under the Copyright Act. In this case, the compilation or arrangement is considered to be an original work, but the government document material used in the compilation remains within the public domain and may be reproduced without permission of the copyright holder.

Broome Community College

Exclusive Rights In Copyrighted Works

The Copyright Act grants exclusive rights to the owner of a copyright to do and to authorize any of the following:

A. to reproduce the copyrighted work in copies or phonorecords;[1]

B. to prepare derivative works based upon the copyrighted work;

C. to distribute copies or phonorecords of the copyrighted work to the public by sale or other transfer of ownership, or by rental, lease, or lending;

D. in the case of literary, musical, dramatic, and choreographic works, pantomimes, motion pictures and other audiovisual works, to perform the copyrighted work publicly;

E. in the case of literary, musical, dramatic, and choreographic works, pantomimes, and pictorial, graphic, or sculptural works, including the individual images of a motion picture or other audiovisual work, to display the copyrighted work publicly.

The owner of the copyright of a copyrighted work has the exclusive right to reproduce and distribute the work. It is important to be aware that the law applies even to material distributed free to students.

A faculty member is responsible for copying done at his or her request, even though the actual copying may be done by another person.

[1] Phonorecord is used here as a special term to underscore the fact that a sound recording (whether on record, tape or disc) is a separate work from the underlying work, and has its own copyright. For purposes of economy, we will use "copy" to mean phonorecord as well, whenever applicable.

Limitations on Exclusive Rights: Fair Use

General

The copyright owner's exclusive reproduction and distribution rights are subject to important exceptions. The fair use exception in Section 107 of the Copyright Act permits copying without the copyright owner's permission for purposes such as criticism, comment, scholarship, research, or teaching and also authorizes the making of multiple copies for classroom use under certain circumstances and where the use is reasonable and not harmful to the rights of the copyright owner.

The Copyright Act does not attempt to specify precisely what uses might be fair, but leaves the determination for case-by-case decision making. Fair use provisions of the law were designed to be widely applied to a variety of educational situations.

In determining whether a particular instance of copying could be considered as a "fair use" of a copyrighted work, a person must consider four factors:

1. the purpose and character of the use, including whether such use is of a commercial nature or is for nonprofit educational purposes;

2. the nature of the copyrighted work;

3. the amount and substantiality of the portion used in relation to the work as a whole;

4. the effect of the use upon the potential market for or value of the copyrighted work.

It is important to remember that assessment of what is and what is not fair use relies on the judgment of the individual and must be made on a case-by-case basis. The following illustrations are meant to offer guidance about what might be considered fair use as we look at the four statutory criteria.

Remember, compliance with the Fair Use Guidelines of the Copyright Act requires a particular instance of copying to meet all four criteria.

1. Purpose and character of the use.

A finding of fair use is more likely if:

a. the use of the copyrighted work is for a nonprofit educational purpose, rather than a commercial purpose (however, a nonprofit educational purpose does not ensure absolutely that the use is fair);

b. no charge is made for the copies (beyond the actual cost of reproduction); and

c. the original and the copy do not serve the same function, e.g., a copy is made to avoid purchasing the original and is then used in place of the original.

2. Nature of the copyrighted work.

A finding of fair use is more likely if the copyrighted work is:

a. a compilation of facts or information rather than a creative or imaginative work;

b. out of print or unavailable for purchase through normal channels;

c. not a consumable work (such as a workbook);

d. not intended for performance or public exhibition (such as a musical score); or

e. a newspaper or periodical (but not a newsletter) containing articles of current interest.

In the context of classroom use, copying from textbooks and other materials prepared primarily for the educational market is less likely to be considered fair use than is copying from materials designed for general public distribution.

3. Amount and substantiality of the material used in relation to the copyrighted work as a whole.

Both the quantity (the amount copied) and the quality (the importance of the portion copied) of the use must be considered. A finding of fair use is more likely if the material copied:

a. is a small portion of the total work; and

b. does not contain a substantial amount of the essence or principle elements of the work.

4. Effect of the use on the potential market for or value of the work.

A finding of fair use is more likely if the use:

a. does not supplant a portion of the market for the work; or

b. stimulates sales of the work.

Appendix B of this handbook contains a series of questions a person wishing to reproduce a copyrighted work should ask to determine whether a particular use can be considered a fair use. We hope that the above illustrations and the questions in Appendix B will help faculty and staff answer everyday questions about reproducing copyrighted materials without permission of the copyright holder. Questions about whether a particular request to photocopy or duplicate an item constitutes fair use which can't be answered by reference to the information in this handbook, should be directed to the Campus Copyright Officer.

Educational Uses of Copyrighted Materials

The legislative history of the Copyright Act clearly indicates an unwillingness to free educational copying from copyright control while, at the same time, recognizing a need for guidance about permissible amounts of photocopying of copyrighted materials for educational purposes.

To offer some guidance, an Agreement on Guidelines for Classroom Copying in Not-for-Profit Educational Institutions (hereafter referred to as Classroom Guidelines) was drawn up by representatives of various educational organizations and included, not as part of the Copyright Act itself, but as part of the legislative history of the Act. These Classroom Guidelines list specific, quantitative standards for minimum (but not maximum) fair use copying, including both single copying by teachers and multiple copying for classroom use. What follows is the "Agreement" in its entirety:

Agreement on Guidelines for Classroom Copying in Not-For-Profit Educational Institutions with Respect to Books and Periodicals

The purpose of the following guidelines is to state the minimum, and not the maximum, standards of educational fair use under section 107 of H.R. 2223. The parties agree that the conditions determining the extent of permissible copying for educational purposes may change in the future; and conversely that in the future other types of copying not permitted under these guidelines may be permissible under revised guidelines.

Moreover, the following statement of guidelines is not intended to limit the types of copying permitted under the standards of fair use under judicial decision and which are stated in Section 107 of the Copyright Revision Bill. There may be instances in which copying which does not fall within the guidelines stated below may nonetheless be permitted under the criteria of fair use.

Guidelines
I. Single Copying for Teachers

A single copy may be made of any of the following by or for a teacher at his or her individual request, for his or her scholarly research, or use in teaching or preparation to teach a class:

A. a chapter from a book;

B. an article from a periodical or newspaper;

C. a short story, short essay or short poem, whether or not from a collective work;

D. a chart, graph, diagram, drawing, cartoon or picture from a book, periodical, or newspaper.

II. Multiple Copies for Classroom Use

Multiple copies (not to exceed in any event more than one copy per pupil in a course) may be made by or for the teacher giving the course for classroom use or discussion, provided that:

A. the copying meets the tests of brevity and spontaneity as defined below; and,

B. meets the cumulative effect test as defined below; and,

C. each copy includes a notice of copyright.

Definitions
Brevity

(i) Poetry: (a) a complete poem if less than 250 words and if printed on not more than two pages, or (b) from a longer poem, an excerpt of not more than 250 words.

(ii) Prose: (a) Either a complete article, story or essay of less than 2,500 words, or (b) an excerpt from any prose work of not more than 1,000 words or 10 percent of the work, whichever is less, but in any event a minimum of 500 words.

[Each of the numerical limits stated in (i) and (ii) above may be expanded to permit the completion of an unfinished line of a poem or of an unfinished prose paragraph.]

(iii) Illustration: One chart, graph, diagram, drawing, cartoon or picture per book or per periodical issue.

(iv) "Special" works: Certain works in poetry, prose or in "poetic prose" which often combine language with illustrations and which are intended sometimes for children and at other times for a more general audience fall short of 2,500 words in their entirety. Paragraph (ii) above notwithstanding, such "special works" may not be reproduced in their entirety; however, an excerpt comprising not more than two of the published pages of such special work and containing not more than 10 percent of the words found in the text thereof, may be reproduced.

Spontaneity

(i) The copying is at the instance and inspiration of the individual teacher.

(ii) The inspiration and decision to use the work and the moment of its use for maximum teaching effectiveness are so close in time that it would be unreasonable to expect a timely reply to a request for permission.

Music and Performance Guidelines

Copying of Music for Classroom Use

Representatives of music educators and music publishers developed a set of specific Guidelines for Educational Uses of Music similar to the Classroom Guidelines developed for books and periodicals. These Music Guidelines are intended to state the minimum standards of educational fair use of music and are part of the legislative history of the Copyright Act.

The Music Guidelines are not intended to limit the types of copying permitted under fair use standards and they recognize that there may be instances of copying which do not fall within their stated parameters, but nonetheless may be determined to be fair use.

Permissible Uses

a. Emergency copying to replace purchased copies which for any reason are not available for an imminent performance provided that purchased replacement copies shall be substituted in due course.

b. For academic purposes other than performance:

- Multiple Copies of excerpts of works may be made, provided that the excerpts do not comprise a part of the whole which would constitute a performable entity, such as a section, movement or aria, but in no case more than 10% of the whole work. The number of copies should be one per student.

- A single copy of a work determined to be out-of-print or unavailable except in a larger work may be made for scholarly research or in preparation for teaching.

c. Printed copies which have been purchased may be edited or simplified provided that the fundamental character of the work is not distorted or the lyrics, if any, altered or lyrics added if none exist.

d. A single copy of recordings of performances by students may be made for evaluation or rehearsal purposes and may be retained by the educational institution or individual instructor.

e. A single phonorecord of a sound recording of copyrighted music may be made from sound recordings owned by an educational institution or individual instructor for the purpose of constructing aural exercises or examinations.

Cumulative Effect

(i) The copying of the material is for only one course in the school in which the copies are made.

(ii) Not more than one short poem, article, story, essay or two excerpts may be copied from the same author, nor more than three from the same collective work or periodical volume during one class term.

(iii) There shall not be more than nine instances of such multiple copying for one course during one class term.

[The limitations stated in (ii) and (iii) above shall not apply to current news periodicals and newspapers and current news sections of other periodicals.]

III. Prohibitions as to I and II Above

Notwithstanding any of the above, the following shall be prohibited:

A. Copying shall not be used to create or to replace or substitute for anthologies, compilations or collective works. Such replacement or substitution may occur whether copies of various works or excerpts therefrom are accumulated or reproduced and used separately.

B. There shall be no copying of or from works intended to be "consumable" in the course of study or of teaching. These include workbooks, exercises, standardized tests and test booklets and answer sheets and like consumable material.

C. Copying shall not:

(a) substitute for the purchase of books, publishers' reprints or periodicals;

(b) be directed by higher authority;

(c) be repeated with respect to the same item by the same teacher from term to term.

D. No charge shall be made to the student beyond the actual cost of the photocopying.

Reproduction of Copyrights worked by Educators and Librarians, Circular 21. Washington, D.C.: Copyright Office, 1992. p. 10-11.

10 11

Prohibited Uses

Examples of music copying which are considered to go beyond fair use are:

a. copying to create, replace or substitute for anthologies, compilations or collective works.

b. copying works intended to be consumable.

c. copying for the purpose of performance, except as an emergency.

d. copying in lieu of purchasing music, except under emergency circumstances or when works are out of print or unavailable.

Faculty and staff should keep in mind that these Music Guidelines are not meant to limit fair use copying which permits copying a single copy of most material for personal use. They also do not prohibit editing a piece of music for personal scholarly pursuits or as a classroom exercise. They do, however, prohibit the making of substantial revisions of a piece of music and distribution or performance of the edited version.

Classroom Performance of Films and Videotapes

The Copyright Act protects audiovisual works such as films and videotapes. The law creates a legal distinction between classroom performances and other public performances or reception of programming in the privacy of one's home. In-classroom performance of a copyrighted film or videotape is permissible under the following conditions:

a. the showing must be by instructors (including guest lecturers) or by students; and

b. the showing of the video tape is in connection with face-to-face teaching activities; and

c. the entire audience is involved in the teaching activity; and

d. the entire audience is in the same room or same general area;

e. the teaching activities are conducted by a non-profit educational institution; and

f. the showing takes place in a classroom or similar place devoted to instruction, such as a school library, gym, auditorium or workshop;

g. the videotape is lawfully made; the person responsible had no reason to believe that the videotape was unlawfully made.

Home Copied Videotapes for Classroom Use

The law makes a distinction between the act of recording a program on videotape in the privacy of one's home and the act of displaying that program in a public space such as a classroom. It is not clear that if a faculty member tapes a program on his/her VCR and shows it in the classroom, such an act would constitute a violation of fair use in an educational setting. Decisions would have to be made on a case-by-case basis, weighing the circumstances of each case against fair use criteria.

Reformatting Films on Videotapes for Classroom Use

Making a derivative copy of a copyrighted work (for example, changing the format of a 16mm film to a videotape) is also a problematic area for higher education. Creating a derivative work under current law is an important exclusive right of the copyright owner. Educators, media specialists, librarians and others often want to change the format of audiovisual materials for convenience of use, purposes of preservation or ease of multiple access. Although some flexibility has been granted to libraries for purposes of archival preservation, it is probably best to assume that the making of derivative works should be done only with prior permission from the copyright owner, or if permission is granted as a written condition of a sales contract.

Classroom Performances of Plays, Musicals, Operas, Sketches, etc.

Faculty and students may perform or display any work in any College sponsored classroom instructional activity for students, their family and social acquaintances without seeking prior permission from the copyright owner or paying a licensing fee. However, if the audience consists primarily of off campus members of the community, the performance or display may not be covered by classroom instruction exemptions and may constitute a copyright infringement. In order to avoid a possible copyright infringement for performances of this type, permission from the copyright owner should be obtained prior to the performance.

Public Performances of Music, Drama, Films, etc.

Nondramatic musical performances - such as dances and concerts - that are under College auspices but not covered by classroom copyright exemptions are covered by blanket licenses obtained by the College from ASCAP and BMI, two of the three major licensing societies.

Musical performances with any dramatic content - and this would include even a single "number" from an opera or musical - may be done outside of the classroom setting only with the advance permission of the copyright holder and the payment of any required fees. The same rule applies to purely dramatic performances, as of plays and pantomimes, and to showings of films. In the case of films, please note that rental of a print from a regular rental agency carries a performance license with it. This is not true of a cassette, and separate permission from the copyright owner must be obtained for airing any cassette in a public performance.

Library Copying

In addition to exercising fair use rights as listed in Section 107 of the Copyright Act, non-profit libraries and archives are authorized to reproduce copyrighted works without permission under the circumstances indicated in Section 108 of the law.

Single copies of works or portions of works may be reproduced and distributed by a library employee if:

- there is no direct or indirect commerical advantage;
- the library or archive is open to the public or available to researchers working in a specific field;
- the copy contains a notice of copyright.

Library rights under Section 108 are for isolated and unrelated reproduction or distribution, e.g., a single copy of the same work may be distributed on separate occasions. Libraries may not engage in or knowingly be a party to the systematic reproduction or distribution of single or multiple copies of copyrighted material. Libraries may, however, participate in interlibrary loan arrangements under certain conditions. These conditions are outlined in the section of this handbook entitled - Library Copying-Interlibrary Loan.

Library Reserve Shelf Use

Photocopying for library reserve use is not mentioned specifically in the Copyright Act. In an attempt to offer guidance to faculty and libraries, the American Library Association issued a recommendation to libraries regarding photocopying for reserve shelf activities. This model policy has been adapted for use by the College's Library and is reproduced below.

At the request of a faculty member, a library may photocopy and place on reserve excerpts from copyrighted works in its collection in accordance with guidelines similar to the Classroom Guidelines for face-to-face teaching discussed earlier in this handbook. The College believes that these guidelines apply to the library reserve shelf to the extent that it functions as an extension of classroom readings or reflects an individual student's right to photocopy for his/her personal scholastic use under the doctrine of fair use. In general, the library may photocopy materials for reserve shelf use for the convenience of students both in preparing class assignments and in pursuing informal educational activities which higher education requires, such as advanced independent study and research.

If the faculty request asks for only one copy to be placed on reserve, the library may photocopy an entire article, or an entire chapter from a book, or an entire poem.

14

Requests for multiple copies on reserve should meet the following guidelines:

a. the amount of material should be reasonable in relation to the total amount of material assigned for one term of a course taking into account the nature of the course, its subject matter and level;

b. the number of copies should be reasonable in light of the number of students enrolled, the difficulty and timing of assignments, and the number of other courses which may assign the same material;

c. the material should contain a notice of copyright;

d. the effect of photocopying the material should not be detrimental to the market for the work. (In general, the library should own at least one copy of the work.)

For example, a faculty member may place on reserve, as a supplement to the course textbook, a reasonable number of copies of articles from academic periodicals or chapters from books.

A reasonable number of copies will in most instances be less than six, but factors such as the length or difficulty of the assignment, the number of enrolled students and the length of time allowed for completion of the assignment may permit more in unusual circumstances.

In addition, a faculty member may also request that multiple copies of photocopied copyrighted material be placed on the reserve shelf if there is insufficient time to obtain permission from the copyright owner. For example, a professor may place on reserve several photocopies of an entire article from a recent issue of TIME magazine or the NEW YORK TIMES in lieu of distributing a copy to each member of the class.

Please keep in mind: if there is any doubt as to whether a particular instance of photocopying can be considered fair use in the reserve shelf context, the copyright owner's permission should be sought. (See Appendix A for advice on how to obtain permission.)

Materials placed on reserve will be returned to the faculty member at the end of each semester.

Photocopying and Duplication Which Require Permission

a. **Repetitive Copying:** The classroom or reserve use of photocopied materials in multiple courses or successive years will normally require advance permission from the copyright owner;

b. **Copying for Profit:** Faculty should not charge students more than the actual cost of photocopying the material;

c. **Consumable Works:** The duplication of works that are consumed in the classroom, such as standardized tests, exercises, and workbooks, normally requires permission from the copyright owner;

15

COMPUTERS AND SOFTWARE

The College has hundreds of stand alone microcomputers. These devices are intended largely for use by a single individual at a time, though they are extremely adaptable and operate in a variety of environments and perform a number of different functions. With the dispersal of microcomputers throughout the College, the use of, and demand for, computer software has increased dramatically. The nature and cost of this electronic technology, and the ease with which it can be reproduced, raises crucial issues about the educational uses of computer software and the rights and responsibilities of educators and administrators to honor and enforce copyright protection of it.

Since the applications for using microcomputers are so diverse, and since the applications are chiefly for single users at a time, responsibility for honoring the copyrights of software manufacturers is in the hands of many individual users and not easily managed by the College. Furthermore, the legal distinction of the "owner," "purchaser," and "operator" of software acquired by the College becomes uncertain under conditions of serial use with software borrowed from the College for authorized applications.

The College maintains an interest in establishing and protecting its rights as lawful owner of any and all software purchased or otherwise acquired for use on its equipment in the ordinary conduct of its mission. At the same time, the College also supports and protects the legal rights of software manufacturers, licensors, and distributors, insofar as the rights and privileges of the College are not abridged.

In exploring the policy issues surrounding copyright and computer software, it is important to understand several sections of the Copyright Act in some detail.

Copyright Protection of Computer Software

The Copyright Act gives significant protection to the creators of computer software. The copyright owner of software has the same exclusive rights as the copyright owner of any other creative and original work in some other format: reproduction, adaptation, distribution, public performance, and public display.

> "As a consequence of these exclusive rights, the copyright owner controls who may prepare duplicate disks, load programs from disks, cause computers to create additional copies within their memories, prepare working and archive copies, alter the functioning of programs, modify program code to run on particular computers, exhibit copies of program code to students and run programs in class. All of these acts involve one or more of the above exclusive rights."[2]

---

² Daniel Brooks, *Copyright and the Educational Uses of Computer Software.* EDUCOM Bulletin, Summer 1985, p. 7.

17

---

d. **Creation of Anthologies as Basic Text Material for a Course:** Creation of a collective work or anthology by photocopying a number of copyrighted articles and excerpts to be purchased and used together as the basic text for a course will, in most instances, require the permission of the copyright holders. Such photocopying is more likely to be considered as a substitute for purchase of a book and thus less likely to be deemed fair use.

Interlibrary Loan

The Copyright Act specifically authorizes the provision of photocopies in lieu of interlibrary loans for single photocopies of articles from periodicals or collections, or of small parts of other copyrighted works without copyright liability. This right is limited, however, by complicated language in the law reflecting a carefully drawn congressional compromise.

One half of the compromise is a provision stating that the right does not extend to the "systematic" reproduction and distribution of copies. The other half is a proviso making it clear that an activity will not be considered "systematic" as long as the library or archives receiving the reproductions does not do so in such "aggregate quantities as to substitute for a subscription to or purchase of the work."

Prior to the enactment of the Copyright Act, library and publisher organizations developed a set of guidelines to assist in interpreting the quoted language of the interlibrary loan proviso.

These guidelines were negotiated with the assistance of the National Commission on New Technological Use of Copyrighted Works (CONTU), and were incorporated into the Congressional conference committee report on the Copyright Act. The CONTU guidelines give the following interpretation:

- with respect to a periodical title (not a given issue of a periodical), the language of the proviso means filling a request of a library or archives within any calendar year for six or more copies of articles published in the periodical within five years prior to the date of the request (periodical articles that are more than five years old were generally considered to be so infrequently requested that they are not covered by the guidelines);

- with respect to all other material, the language of the proviso means filling requests of a single requesting entity within any calendar year for six or more copies of any given copyrighted work.

The law recognized that photocopies may be provided in lieu of interlibrary loans. In the typical case, the provision of the photocopy serves exactly the same purpose as a loan of the work itself, and simply reduces the risk of loss or damage in transit and reduces the transaction cost.

Owning a Copy Versus Licensing a Copy

The issue of ownership of a computer program is complicated by the fact that most computer software is not sold outright, but is "licensed" to a user by a vendor. Frequently software comes in a clear plastic wrapper through which the user can read a warning that breaking the wrapper and opening the package constitutes acceptance of the terms of the conditions of the licensing agreement. The legality and binding nature of these licensing agreements have not been sufficiently tested in the courts. In the absence of evidence to the contrary, it is wise to assume that licensing agreements may bind the user to the terms of that agreement and that these terms may take precedence over other rights granted by the Copyright Act.

Fair Use of Computer Software

As we have seen in earlier discussions of copyright protection for works in other formats, e.g. books, periodicals, music, video, etc., the fair use provision of the Copyright Act may permit some exceptions to the exclusive rights of the copyright owner.

Although fair use was discussed earlier in this handbook, it is worth repeating some key points here. The fair use provision permits copying without the copyright owner's permission for purposes such as criticism, comment, scholarship, research, and teaching.

In order to decide if a particular instance of copying could be considered as a "fair use" of a copyrighted work, all four criteria must be considered and met:

1) the purpose and character of the use, including if the use is non-profit educational purposes,

2) the nature of the copyrighted work,

3) the amount and substantiality of the portion,

4) the effect of the use on the potential market or value of the copyrighted work.

Although the assessment of what is and is not fair use relies on the judgment of the individual and must be made on a case-by-case basis, the application of fair use in questions about computer software is particularly problematic.

The attorney and Director of the Computer Law Association argued in a recent article that since computer programs must be copied in their entirety to be useful, and since fair use copying means copying only a small part in relation to the whole, the quantitative test for fair use copying cannot apply. Similarly, it is unlikely that reproducing a software program in its entirety can pass the market effect test. If copying is done in lieu of purchasing additional copies, then the copying damages the

---

Ownership of copyright, and any one or more of the exclusive rights, can only be acquired by someone other than the author: 1) by written transfers from the author (e.g. purchase or license agreements) or 2) by operation of law under the "works for hire" doctrine (i.e., employers are the "authors" of the works of their employees produced "within the scope" of their employment or for works which are "specially produced within the scope" of their employment). (See Section 201b of the Copyright Act for a more complete explanation of the "works for hire" exception.)

Ownership of Copyright Versus Ownership of a Copy

The law distinguishes between ownership of copyright and ownership of a copy. Under Section 109 of the Copyright Act "the owner of a particular copy...lawfully made...or any person authorized by the owner, is entitled, without the authority of the copyright owner, to sell or otherwise dispose of that copy.

With the first sale of a given copy which has been lawfully made, the copyright owner's exclusive right to distribute the copy to the public, or to display the work publicly, terminates as to that given copy. Therefore, if a faculty member or a student buys a copy of a software package, that copy can be legally resold, lent to someone else, displayed, or destroyed, but it cannot be legally copied except under the specific condition delineated in Section 117 of the Copyright Act. Section 117 states:

It is not an infringement for the owner of a copy of a computer program to make or authorize the making of another copy or adaptation of a computer program provided:

A) that such a new copy or adaptation is created as an essential step in the utilization of the computer program in conjunction with a machine and that it is used in no other manner, or

B) that the new copy or adaptation is for archival purposes only and that all archival copies are destroyed in the event that continued possession of the computer program should cease to be rightful.

Any exact copies prepared in accordance with the provisions of this section may be leased, sold, or otherwise transferred, along with the copy from which copies were prepared, only as part of the lease, sale, or other transfer of all rights in the program. Adaptations so prepared may be transferred only with the authorization of the copyright owner.

Section 117 gives the owner of a copy permission to do the copying necessary to use the software without infringing upon the exclusive rights of the copyright owner. It does not give the owner of a copy the right to duplicate the software for others to use.

market for the work and has an adverse impact on the copyright owners. The attorney concluded,

"If the copies made have the effect of increasing the number of simultaneous users of the purchased programs, the fair use and computer programs sections of the Copyright Act are not satisfactory defenses to charges of infringement.... However, serial use of the same owned original by more than one person is probably permissible.

...But be careful. Not all program disks are owned copies. Some are leased. Some are loaned.... The loan agreement, or trade secret license control what the user may do with the original."[3]

As is apparent from the above discussion, fair use concepts may not be readily applicable to instances of copying computer software and may not provide sufficient justification for software copying.

College Statement on Computer Software Copyright

Respect for intellectual labor and creativity is vital to academic discourse and enterprise. This principle applies to works of all authors and publishers in all media. It encompasses respect for the right to acknowledgment, right to privacy, and right to determine the form, manner, and terms of publication and distribution.

The College, in accordance with the provisions of the Copyright Act, encourages the authorized copying of rightfully owned, leased, or rented computer software and/or documentation to the fullest extent allowed by law. The College explicitly prohibits the making, using and distributing of unauthorized and illegal copies of copyrighted computer software.

Broome Community College

[3]Daniel Brooks, *Copyright and the Educational Uses of Computer Software.* EDUCOM Bulletin, Summer 1985, p. 13.

Audiovisual Materials

Media Center/TV Studio/Graphics

College policy on duplication of copyrighted material is governed by the provisions of the Copyright Act and informed by the Classroom Guidelines and the Guidelines for Off-Air Taping of Copyrighted Works for Educational Use (hereafter referred to as the Off-Air Taping Guidelines). College general procedure is listed below. Questions concerning duplication of audiotapes, videotapes, films, etc., not answered here should be referred to the Campus Copyright Officer.

A. As a general statement of procedure, the College will not copy any copyrighted material as a substitute for purchasing the material at a fair market price.

B. No audio or video tapes are duplicated by the College unless they are originated by the client or a written release from the copyright owner is presented at the time of the request for duplication. This procedure also applies to the transfer of motion pictures or slides to videotape.

C. The College will reproduce copyrighted graphics material within the criteria established by the fair use provisions of the copyright law.

Minimally, the College will make a single photocopy or typeset copy of one page of a publication. For requests, which exceed the minimum, each request must be weighed against fair use criteria to determine whether or not it may be considered as educational fair use. If a request is believed to exceed the limits of fair use, it will not be duplicated. Examples of requests which might exceed fair use include requests for multiple copies of a single graphic item or for a single copy of a number of illustrations in one publication. These types of requests should be accompanied by written permission to duplicate from the copyright owner.

Videotapes — Off-Air Taping Guidelines

The following guidelines reflect a negotiated consensus as to the application of "fair use" to the recording, retention and use of television broadcast programs for educational purposes. They specify periods of retention and use of off-air recordings in classrooms and similar places devoted to instruction and for home-bound instruction. The purpose of establishing these guidelines is to provide standards for both owners and users of copyrighted television programs. The College adheres to these guidelines.

A. The guidelines were developed to apply only to off-air recording by non-profit educational institutions.

B. A broadcast program may be recorded off-air simultaneously with broadcast transmission (including simultaneous cable retransmission) and retained by a non-profit educational institution for a period not to exceed the first forty-five (45) consecutive calendar days after date of recording. Upon

distribution system, laser camera, or microwave system. Such rights should be negotiated with the producer or distributor at the time of purchase by the media services coordinator. Faculty who wish to use these materials in the ways excluded by the original license, should contact the Media Services Coordinator as soon as they identify them.

Duplication of Sound Recordings

The College provides services for duplication of audio tapes. These services are governed by the Copyright Act and rules, regulations and guidelines of the State University of New York.

Public Law 94-553, generally referred to as the Copyright Act, has two sections which are applicable to the above named services:

Section 107 (Fair Use), generally speaking, allows copying without permission from, or payment to, the copyright owner where the use is reasonable and not harmful to the rights of the copyright owner.

Section 108 (Reproduction by Libraries and Archives) deals with a variety of situations involving photocopying and other forms of duplication by libraries and archives. Briefly stated the issues addressed are: libraries and archives may photocopy or duplicate materials when fair use has been considered; individuals or institutions doing such copying may be held liable and the multiple and systematic copying is not extended under this section.

For further clarification see the full text of PL94-553; the General Guide to the Copyright Act of 1976, Copyright Office Library Congress, Washington, D.C., 1977.

Copies of audiotapes will be made upon request of library patrons if, in the judgment of the Copyright Officer, all applicable sections of the Copyright Act are satisfied. The general guidelines are as follows:

1. The request falls within educational fair use criteria;

2. The reproduction and/or distribution is made without any purpose of direct or indirect commercial advantage to the requestor;

3. The reproduction and/or distribution of the works includes a notice of copyright;

4. The reproduction and/or distribution is of a single copy that is isolated and unrelated to any other reproduction or distribution; and,

5. A Copy Service request is completed and signed by the person requesting the copy.

conclusion of this retention period, all off-air recordings must be erased or destroyed immediately. "Broadcast programs" are television programs transmitted by television stations for reception by the general public without charge.

C. Off-air recordings may be used once by individual teachers in the course of relevant teaching activities, and repeated once only when instructional reinforcement is necessary, in classrooms and similar places devoted to instruction within a single building, cluster or campus, as well as in the homes of students receiving formalized home instruction, during the first ten (10) consecutive school days in the forty-five (45) calendar day retention period. "School days" are school session days - not counting weekends, holidays, vacations, examination periods, or other scheduled interruptions - within the forty-five (45) calendar day retention period.

D. Off-air recordings may be made only at the request of and used by individual teachers, and may not be regularly recorded in anticipation of requests. No broadcast program may be recorded off-air more than once at the request of the same teacher, regardless of the number of times the program may be broadcast.

E. After the first ten (10) consecutive school days, off-air recordings may be used up to the end of the forty-five (45) calendar day retention period only for teacher evaluation purposes, i.e., to determine whether or not to include the broadcast program in the teaching curriculum, and may not be used in the recording institution for student exhibition or any other non-evaluation purpose without authorization.

F. Off-air recordings need not be used in their entirety, but the recorded programs may not be altered from their original content. Off-air programs may not be physically or electronically combined or merged to constitute teaching anthologies or compilations.

G. All copies of off-air recordings must include the copyright notice on the broadcast program as recorded.

H. Educational institutions are expected to establish appropriate control procedures to maintain the integrity of these guidelines.

Film Service

The LRC houses a collection of 16mm films and video cassettes along with other media titles in various formats.

The vast majority of the collection was purchased with life-of-the-print rights which allow the performance of the print in face-to-face teaching; this also allows individual students and faculty to view these materials for their own scholarship and research. It does not allow for the transmission of these materials through a film-chain, video

Procedures Regarding the Reproduction of Material on Campus

The following procedures have been established to protect the College and its employees from litigation regarding the infringement of copyright law. It is further expected that College employees will self regulate their use of production and reproduction equipment to which they have access so as not to infringe upon the property rights of copyright owners.

The Publications Center

The BCC Publications Center will not accept for reprint in College publications any copyrighted material unless it conforms to the Fair Use Guidelines or the College department has secured written permission from the copyright owner.

When submitting material protected by the copyright law to the Publications Center, be sure to attach a copy of the permission to copy agreement supplied by the copyright owner.

If permission has not been obtained, please provide written justification based on the Fair Use Guidelines.

The Publications Center reserves the right to refuse to accept a request to reproduce copyrighted material in College publications if fulfillment of the request would involve violation of copyright law.

The Copy Center

The BCC Copy Center will not accept for reprint any copyrighted material unless it conforms to the Fair Use Guidelines or the College department has secured written permission from the copyright owner.

When submitting material protected by the copyright law to the Copy Center, be sure to sign the Copy Center Requisition for Copy/Printing Form. Your signature certifies that the material is either not copyrighted or if it is that it meets Fair Use Criteria or you have obtained permission from the copyright owner.

The Computer Center

Software for computers is included under the literary works category of the copyright guidelines. The license agreement of the specific program must be consulted. Generally, Section 117, as amended in 1980, permits the owner of a program to make a backup copy to be used only if the original fails, to make adaptations necessary to use the program correctly, and to add features to the program, as long as it is not sold or given away without the author's permission. Fair Use Guidelines do not apply to computer programs.

Only the producer or copyright owner has the right to the reproduction of copies, production of derivative works (for various machines), distribution of copies, performance of a work if audiovisual (such as multimedia), and display of a work. In addition, making copies of manuals or documentation without permission or purchase is an infringement.

Examples of audio recordings which may be copied:

- lecture tapes;
- note tapes;
- audiotapes which are made at the College for the visually impaired;
- audiotapes which are owned by the Library and need to be copied to be preserved; (the Library must supply written proof that a copy cannot be obtained at a fair price.)
- audiotapes which are accompanied by a permission to copy letter from the copyright holder.

Examples of audio recordings which may not be copied:

- music and spoken word recordings which are available for purchase from commerical sources;
- compilations of sound recordings.

Copies of sound recordings will be accepted for reserve listening if:

- all applicable sections of the Copyright Act are satisfied;
- a written letter of permission from the copyright holder is presented and filed with the Library for each reproduction of a sound recording placed on reserve;
- this sound recording was commercially prepared and is on original recording material.

Broome Community College

The Learning Resources Center
Photocopier Service:

Photocopier services within the Learning Resources Center (LRC) are provided for individual use by staff, students, faculty, and the general public. Photocopies made must follow the Fair Use Guidelines as defined by single copying for teachers. The following notice is displayed at each LRC photocopier:

Notice: The copyright law of the United States (Title 17 U.S. Code) governs the making of photocopies or other reproductions of copyrighted material. The person using this equipment is liable for any infringement.

A staff bypass key is available for the benefit of campus staff needing photocopier access within the LRC. Copies made with this bypass key must follow the Fair Use Guidelines as defined by single copying for teachers. The following notice is displayed with the bypass key:

Warning Concerning Copyright Restrictions

The copyright law of the United States (Title 17, United States Code) governs the making of photocopies or other reproductions of copyrighted material.

Under certain conditions specified in the law, libraries and archives are authorized to furnish a photocopy or other reproduction. One of these specified conditions is that the photocopy or reproduction is not to be "used for any purpose other than private study, scholarship, or research." If a user makes a request for, or later uses, a photocopy or reproduction for purposes in excess of the Fair Use Criteria, that user may be liable for copyright infringement.

This institution reserves the right to refuse to accept a copying order if, in its judgment, fulfillment of the order would involve violation of copyright law.

Broome Community College

26

Broome Community College
P.O. Box 1017
Binghamton, NY 13902

COPYRIGHT PERMISSION REQUEST FOR DUPLICATION OR ADAPTATION

To: _____ From: _____

Date: _____

We hereby request permission to duplicate, adapt, or use copyrighted materials for the project described below. This project will be used exclusively for educational purposes, with no direct or indirect commercial advantage, and will include credit for your work.

Title of Copyrighted Material: _____

Author: _____

Publisher: _____ Copyright Date: _____

Material to be duplicated or adapted: _____

Type of reproduction or adaptation: _____

Number of copies: _____

Use to be made of material: _____

Distribution of copies: _____

Please indicate your permission below and return this form within two weeks from the above date. A return envelope is enclosed for your convenience.

☐ Permission granted.

☐ Permission granted with the following restrictions: _____

☐ Permission denied. (If so, is there another means by which we can obtain this material for our project?)

☐ Alternate Source: _____

Name (Printed) _____ Title _____

Signature _____ Date _____

27

The Campus Store

The Campus Store is the source on campus for creating multiple copies of course material, lab manuals and other custom teaching aids for sale to students.

The Campus Store, a division of the Faculty-Student Association, agrees with the BCC Board of Trustee Policy on copyright, and therefore requires the same adherence to the Copyright Law of the United States (Title 17 U.S. Code).

When submitting course material packets to the Campus Store for publication, please fill out the appropriate requisition forms available from the Campus Store (samples follow).

The Campus Store reserves the right to refuse a copying request if fulfillment of the order would involve violation of copyright law.

Broome Community College

BCC Broome Community College

The Campus Store
Faculty-Student Association
of Broome Community College, Inc.

Textbook Requisition & Approval For Photocopied Course Material

Semester: _____   Course #(s): _____

Instructor(s): _____

This form requests the publication of classroom materials by the BCC Campus Store. Materials will be packaged as requested and will be sold to BCC students from the regular textbook shelves.

We cannot promise that this material will be available for student purchase the first date of instruction if this material does not meet the semester deadline for submission of text requisitions.

In order to provide the most legible copies, we prefer to use the original material. In cases where the original material is not available, please provide the best possible copy.

Please fill out one (1) form for each title to be printed.

Please fill in the following information as you would like to see it appear on the cover:

Course # _____   Author: _____
Title: _____   Ed/Yr: _____

Please check the appropriate selections for finished package:

☐ Copy on one side of page	☐ Copy on both sides of page
☐ Follow copy instructions on individual pages	☐ Staple
☐ Comb binding	☐ Three hole punched
☐ Two pocket folder	☐ Three ring binder
☐ Laminated front & back cover	☐ Royalty $ _____ per copy
☐ Heavy coverstock front & back	☐ Add On $ _____ per copy
	☐ Other

In addition, is there any copyrighted material contained in the master to be photocopied?   ☐ Yes   ☐ No

If you answered yes to the above question, the copyrighted material MUST be disclosed and the attached Copyright Infringement Release MUST be completed.

Before the BCC Campus Store will accept photocopied course material, the following approval must be obtained:

Approved by: _____   _____
                (Department Chairperson)   (Date)

(Please keep a photocopy of this completed form for your files and return the original to the BCC Campus Store.)
9/93

Copyright Infringement Release

BCC — Broome Community College
The Campus Store
Faculty-Student Association
of Broome Community College, Inc.

Prior to acceptance of any photocopied copyrighted materials from faculty for resale to students, the faculty member presenting the materials must supply the information requested below and sign and date the completed form.

I, _____ , a member of the faculty of Broome Community College have

delivered to the BCC Campus Store a master entitled: _____

to be photocopied for resale to students in course # _____ which includes certain

photocopies of copyrighted material (entitled) (excerpted from) _____

I certify that each of these photocopies contains a page on which a notice of the copyright appears.

IMPORTANT:

Have you obtained, from the publisher or copyright owner, permission to make multiple copies of the copyrighted materials you have requested this store to sell to your students? ☐ Yes ☐ No

If yes, attach a copy of the permission document to this release.

If no, do you wish to have the BCC Campus Store secure permission and bill the cost to the Academic Department? ☐ Yes ☐ No

I, _____ , a member of the faculty of Broome Community College, do hereby agree to hold harmless the Faculty-Student Association of Broome Community College Inc., its employees and agents, and to indemnify it from any claim, liability, expenses, damages, or costs of any nature incurred in connection with a charge of copyright infringement arising out of the sale of the copyrighted materials described above.

_____ (Faculty Signature) _____ (Date)

_____ (Chairperson Signature) _____ (Date)

Further, if it is necessary to pay royalties to copy this material it will be the decision of the Dean of your Division to authorize the printing of this material. If permission is granted by the Dean, royalties will be added as a fee to each copy printed for resale.

_____ (Dean) _____ (Date)

(Please keep a photocopy of this completed form for your files and return the original to the BCC Campus Store.)

9/93

Printing Quantity

BCC — Broome Community College
The Campus Store
Faculty-Student Association
of Broome Community College, Inc.

Expected Enrollment _____

Unlike regular textbooks, photocopied packages or manuals cannot be returned as overstock to Publishers for a refund at the end of the semester. Therefore, it is essential that you be as exact with your enrollment figures as possible. In determining quantity to print, please keep in mind that when a manual is revised or updated, overstock copies of the outdated manuals will be charged to the academic department.

Number of pages in master: _____

Intended use (check one): ☐ Required ☐ Optional

Departments are entitled to desk copies of the photocopied material free of charge. The cost for these free copies will be factored into the student purchase price for the manual. Therefore, it is essential that the number of copies needed for the upcoming semester be indicated below. Additional copies above the number requested below may be purchased or billed to the Academic Department.

We need _____ copies for faculty teaching this course.

Special Instructions/Notes: _____

_____ (Faculty Signature) _____ (Date)

_____ (Chairperson Signature) _____ (Date)

(Please keep a photocopy of this completed form for your files and return the original to the BCC Campus Store.)

9/93

Appendix A: Writing for Permission and Sample Letter

How to Obtain Permission

When a use of photocopied material requires that you request permission, you should communicate complete and accurate information to the copyright owner. The American Association of Publishers suggests that the following information be included in a permission request letter in order to expedite the process:

1. Title, author and/or editor, and edition of materials to be duplicated.

2. Exact material to be used — giving amount; page numbers; chapters; and, if possible, a photocopy of the material.

3. Number of copies to be made.

4. Use to be made of duplicated materials.

5. Form of distribution (classroom, newsletter, etc.).

6. Whether or not the material is to be sold.

7. Type of reprint (ditto, photography, offset, typeset).

The request should be sent, together with a self-addressed return envelope, to the permissions department of the publisher in question. If the address of the publisher does not appear at the front of the material, it may be readily obtained through the assistance of LRC reference librarians.

The process of granting permission requires time for the publisher to check the status of the copyright and to evaluate the nature of the request. It is advisable, therefore, to allow enough lead time to obtain permission before the materials are needed. In some instances, the publisher may assess a fee for the permission. It is not inappropriate to pass this fee on to the students who receive copies of the photocopied material.

A sample form requesting Permission to Copy follows:

Broome Community College

BCC Broome Community College
P.O. Box 1017
Binghamton, NY 13902

COPYRIGHT PERMISSION REQUEST FOR LIBRARY RESERVE

To: _____ From: _____
Date: _____

We hereby request permission to make copies of the following information in order to place it on reserve in the Learning Resources Center at Broome Community College.

Author or Editor: _____

Article or Chapter Title: _____

Periodical or Book Title: _____

For Periodical - Volume # _____ Issue date _____ Pages _____ ISSN _____

For Book - Copyright date _____ Pages _____ ISBN _____

Number of copies to be placed on reserve: _____

Time item will remain on reserve: _____

These copies will be used exclusively for educational purposes, with no direct or indirect commercial advantage, and will include notice of copyright.

Please indicate your permission below and return this form within two weeks from the above date. A return envelope is enclosed for your convenience.

☐ Permission granted.

☐ Permission granted with the following restrictions: _____

☐ Permission denied. (If so, is there another means by which we can make this material available to a large number of students?) ☐ Alternate Source: _____

Name (Typed) _____ Position _____

Signature _____ Date _____

Appendix B: Questions to Ask in the Determination of Fair Use

1. *How much of the copyrighted work is to be copied?*

   As a general rule, the more of a particular book or periodical copied, the less likely it is that it is fair use. Copying should never substitute for purchasing an item.

2. *Is the request for a single copy or for multiple copies?*

   It is more difficult to justify multiple copies as fair use except for classroom teaching purposes.

3. *How will copying affect the market for the original work?*

   If the copy is meant to substitute for the original, then the request is probably not fair use, unless the copy is to be used for archival or back-up purposes.

4. *What is the nature and format of the work to be copied?*

   Is the request to copy for a chapter of a book, an article in a periodical, an audiotape, picture, slide, etc.? Creating an anthology of articles from a variety of periodicals, copying an entire book, record or audiotape is probably not fair use.

5. *What is the type of use to which the copy will be put?*

   Fair use includes copying material for individual study and research and copying for classroom instruction under many circumstances.

6. *What is the relative value of the work or the copy(ies) made?*

   If the item is expensive, copying it will have greater adverse affect on the market for the original than if the cost of the original is negligible.

7. *Is the request for a copy a substitute for purchasing the original?*

   If yes, the request cannot be considered fair use.

8. *Is the requestor charging money for the copy?*

   If any charge beyond the actual cost of duplication is intended, the request cannot qualify as fair use.

9. *What is the intended distribution of the copy?*

   If distribution of the copies will affect adversely the market for the original, the request cannot be considered fair use.

10. *Is the copyrighted source acknowledged on the copy(ies)?*

    Fair use requires a copyright notice on every copy.

34

Broome Community College

Appendix C: Questions about Computers and Software

EDUCOM has prepared the following questions and answers which may serve as a quick summary to the information presented in the Computers and Software section of this handbook.

1. *What do I need to know about software in the U.S. Copyright Act?*

   Unless it has been placed in the public domain, software is protected by copyright law. The owner of a copyright holds exclusive right to the reproduction and distribution of his or her work. Therefore, it is illegal to duplicate or distribute software or its documentation without the permission of the copyright owner. If you have purchased your copy, however, you may make a back-up for your own use in case the original is destroyed or fails to work.

2. *Can I loan software I have purchased myself?*

   If your software came with a clearly visible license agreement, or if you signed a registration card, read the license carefully before you use the software. Some licenses may restrict use to a specific computer. Copyright law does not permit you to run your software on two or more computers simultaneously unless the license agreement specifically allows it. It may, however, be legal to loan your software to a friend temporarily as long as you do not keep a copy.

3. *If software is not copy-protected, do I have the right to copy it?*

   Lack of copy-protection does not constitute permission to copy software in order to share or sell it. "Non-copy-protected" software enables you to protect your investment by making a back-up copy. In offering non-copy-protected software to you, the developer or publisher has demonstrated significant trust in your integrity.

4. *May I copy software that is available through facilities on my campus, so that I can use it more conveniently in my own room?*

   Software acquired by colleges and universities is usually licensed. The licenses restrict how and where the software may be legally used by members of the community. This applies to software installed on hard disks in microcomputer clusters, software distributed on disks by a campus lending library, and software available on a campus mainframe or network. Some institutional licenses permit copying for certain purposes. Consult your campus authorities if you are unsure about the use of a particular software product.

5. *Isn't it legally "fair use" to copy software if the purpose in sharing it is purely educational?*

   No. It is illegal for a faculty member or student to copy software for distribution among the members of a class, without permission of the author or publisher.

35

COPYRIGHT LAW

GUIDE

FOR LIBRARY

STAFF AND USERS

Tallahassee Community College

Prepared by

Division of Library Services

Tallahassee Community College

July 1995

COPYRIGHT LAW
Table of Contents

COPYRIGHT LAW

INTRODUCTION

At the time the Copyright Law of 1976 went into effect, a guide was prepared by the Division of Library Services in response to numerous requests concerning what would be permissible under the law. This revision of the division's guide has been designed to provide library staff and users with a reference to those parts of the copyright law that apply to library materials. As noted in the original publication, no one knows the answers to all of the questions raised by the law, particularly in the areas of media and information technologies. Moreover, court cases such as the recent case of the American Geophysical Union, et al., vs. Texaco, Inc. continue to define copyright issues in a variety of settings. Amendments passed by Congress through 1993 have been included but the law continues to evolve and is subject to new interpretations.

This guide is divided into four sections: an Overview, Fair Use, Library Applications, and Obtaining Permission. Most of the text has been taken from the actual law and the guidelines that support it. While this makes the text somewhat cumbersome, the reader is working with the original statements, not someone's interpretation (of which there are a great many). For persons interested in reviewing the law for themselves, a bibliography of helpful titles has been attached. In addition, the Director has collect articles, books and other materials about copyright and anyone is welcome to browse through them.

Please note: THIS DOCUMENT SHOULD NOT BE CONSTRUED AS LEGAL ADVICE. As mentioned above, the text relies heavily on the law itself and those guidelines developed at the request of Congress and included in the House and Senate documents. There is a considerable body of interpretive material and unofficial guidelines that have been developed since 1978; however the legal status of much of this material is unknown and has not been included except where noted. There are also a number of other sections of the law pertaining to television broadcasting, public performances, certain uses of music, copyright ownership and transfer, copyright notice, deposit and registration, manufacturing requirements and importation, copyright office, etc. that are not addressed here.

Section 101 of the law as well as other sections such as 111(f) contain definitions of terms as used in the law. It is important in reading the law to understand how it defines such terms as literary works. motion pictures, pictorial. graphic and sculptural works, and local service area.

Lastly, it is important to understand that most publishers and producers are strong defenders of their rights under the copyright law. Producers of media such as film, video, etc. were sometimes reluctant participants in the bargaining processes of the guidelines and indeed some groups rejected the guidelines. Interpretations of fair use and what is a negligible portion particularly in the area of media may vary substantially between user and producer.

Moreover, publishers of format oriented materials, such as West Publishing Corporation. produce reference works and databases that contain materials in the public domain, but whose format is copyrighted. Because of the dual nature of public domain/copyrighted format these publishers guard that copyright jealously and will prosecute violators without fail.

OVERVIEW

Congress passed the first copyright law in 1790. Since then the copyright law has been completely revised five times and amended many more times. Public Law 94-553, the first general revision of the copyright statute since 1909, was enacted into law October of 1976 and became effective January 1, 1978. This law has been described as a "compromise" bill since it seeks to balance the rights of authors and artists and the needs of society.

Copyright definition: Copyright protection subsists in original works of authorship fixed in any tangible medium of expression from which they can be perceived, reproduced or otherwise communicated, either directly or with the aid of a machine or device. Works of authorship include the following categories:
1. literary works
2. musical works, including any accompanying words
3. dramatic works, including any accompanying music
4. pantomimes and choreographic works
5. pictorial, graphic and sculptural works
6. motion pictures and other audiovisual works
7. sound recordings, and
8. architectural works.   #17 USC Section 102

Authors rights: an author has exclusive rights to do and authorize any of the following:
1. to reproduce the work in copies or phonorecords;

2

2. to prepare derivative works based on the copyrighted work;

3. to distribute copies or phonorecords of the work by sale to the public or other transfer of ownership, or by rental, lease or lending;

4. to perform literary, musical, dramatic and choreographic works, pantomimes and motion pictures and other audiovisual works publicly;

5. to display literary, musical, dramatic and choreographic works, pantomimes and pictorial, graphic or sculptural works, including the individual images of a motion picture or other audiovisual work publicly. #17 USC Section 106

Liability:
Liabilities: $500.00 to $20,000 per infringement. If proven law broken by willful intent, statutory penalty may be raised to $100,000.

$500.00 to $250,000 per infringement and/or 1-5 years imprisonment if found guilty of willfully infringing the law for private or commercial gain.   #17 USC Section 501-511

Note: Court shall waive the statutory damages of an employee of a non-profit educational institution or library where the infringer can prove that s/he had believed and had reasonable grounds for believing that his or her use of the copyrighted material was a fair use under Section 107. This does not eliminate the possibility of a civil suit.   #17 USC Section 504(c)(2)

FAIR USE

The Copyright Law attempts to balance the protection of the rights of the author with the needs of society. Even though the author or creator is given certain specific rights under Section 106 of the law, Section 107 begins to set some limitations on those rights followed, in other sections, by specific exemptions granted for particular situations.

This section states that fair use of a copyrighted work including such use by reproduction of copies or phonorecords or by any other means specified by that section for purposes such as criticism, comment, news reporting, teaching, scholarship or research is not an infringement of copyright.

Criteria and Guidelines: The courts use the following four criteria to determine Fair Use:

1. the purpose and character of the use, including whether such use is of a commercial nature or is for nonprofit educational purposes;

2. the nature of the copyrighted work;

3

3. the amount and substantiality of the portion used in relation to the copyrighted work as a whole; and

4. the effect of the use upon the potential market for or value of the copyrighted work.   #17 USC Section 107

Special Guidelines for Classroom Copying: The Fair Use section of the copyright law is interpreted by the "Agreement on Guidelines for Classroom Copying in Not for Profit Educational Institutions with Respect to Books and Periodicals". The guidelines, developed by a committee of authors, publishers, and educators and endorsed by the U.S. House of Representatives, apply to teaching and research in nonprofit educational institutions. These guidelines are summarized below. For a copy of the letter including the guidelines see Vleck, Appendix A.

1. Single copying by teachers

A teacher may make a single copy of any of the following for his or her research, lesson preparation or use in teaching.

a. A chapter of a book
b. An article from a periodical or newspaper
c. A short story, short essay or short poem
d. A chart, graph, diagram, cartoon or picture from a book, periodical or newspaper. More than one illustration can be copied if they are included in a chapter or articles being copied.

2. Multiple copies for classroom use

One copy can be made for each student in a class when the following conditions are met:

a. A complete poem if it is less than 250 words and printed on not more than two pages, or an except of not more than 250 words.
b. A complete article, story or essay of less than 2,500 words or an excerpt not more than 1,000 words, from a larger printed work not to exceed 10% of the whole, whichever of the preceding is less.
c. One chart, graph, diagram, cartoon or picture per book or periodical issue. Copyrighted, syndicated cartoon characters may not be reproduced.
d. Special works combining prose, poetry and illustrations. These include children's picture books and comic books which combine illustrations with a limited text. Copying these works is limited to two pages provided that the

4

pages do not included more than 10% of the words in the work.
    e. All of the above must bear the copyright notice.

3. <u>Limits to the above</u>

    a. Copying must be at the request or inspiration of the individual teacher.
    b. The inspiration to use a material and the time when needed for use does not allow purchasing or seeking permission. This requirement disallows repeated use at a later date.
    c. The copies are used in only one course in the institution.
    d. Only one work may be copied from a single author.
    e. No more than three authors may be copied from a collected work or periodical volume (not issue) during one class term.
    f. No more than 9 instances of such multiple copying in one class term.
    g. Copying may not be used to create anthologies, compilations or collective works,
    h. Consumable works i.e. workbooks, exercises, standardized tests, test booklets and answer sheets may not be copied.
    i. Copying shall not substitute for purchases, be directed by a higher authority, or be requested by the same instructor without permission from the copyright owner.
    j. No charge for copies shall be made to students beyond the actual cost of photocopying.

Specific Guidelines for Nonprint Materials: Any discussion of Fair Use must include a discussion of the guidelines developed for media.

1. <u>Music</u>

    Fair Use guidelines were developed by the Music Publishers' Association, the National Music Publisher's Association, the Music Educators' National Conference, the National Association of Schools of Music, and the Ad Hoc Committee on Copyright Law Revision and incorporated into the House Report of the 94th Congress.

    The guidelines state the minimum and not the maximum standards for educational fair use and are not intended to limit the types of copying permitted under the standards of fair use.

    A. Permissible Uses
    1. Emergency copying to replace purchased copies which for any reason are not available for an imminent performance provided purchased replacement copies shall be substituted in due course.
    2. For academic purposes other than performance, single or multiple

5

copies of excerpts of works may be made, provided that the excerpts do not comprise a part of the whole which would constitute a performable unit such as a selection, movement or aria, but in no case more than 10% of the whole work. The number of copies shall not exceed one copy per pupil.

3. Printed copies which have been purchased may be edited or simplified provided that the fundamental character of the work is not distorted or the lyrics, if any, altered or lyrics added if none exist.

4. A single copy of recordings of performances by students may be made for evaluation or rehearsal purposes and may be retained by the educational institution or individual teacher.

5. A single copy of a sound recording (such as a tape, disk, or cassette) of copyrighted music may be made from sound recordings owned by an educational institution or an individual teacher for the purpose of constructing aural exercises or examinations and may be retained by the educational institution or individual teacher. (This pertains only to the copyright of the music itself and not to any copyright which may exist in the sound recording.)

B. Prohibitions
1. Copying to create or replace or substitute for anthologies, compilations or collective works.

2. Copying of or from works intended to be "consumable" in the course of study or of teaching such as workbooks, exercises, standardized texts and answer sheets and like material.

3. Copying for the purpose of performance, except as in A(1) above.

4. Copying for the purpose of substituting for the purchase of music, except as in A(1)and A(2) above.

5. Copying without inclusion of the copyright notice which appears on the printed copy.   Guidelines for Educational uses of Music

Some authorities state the these guidelines have been accepted as the intent of the Fair Use (Section 107) of the Copyright Act as pertains to educational uses of music (Becker, p. 16).

2. Audio Visual Materials

Films, videotapes and other audio visual materials may not be copied or altered unless the copying meets the four tests for fair use. At present no guidelines have been developed to cover this kind of copying and the issue is not addressed in the law. In general, copying, altering or transferring a program to another format requires written permission.

a. In-classroom use: In-classroom use of copyrighted audio visual materials is permissible if the performance or display of a work by instructors or pupils is in the course of face-to-face teaching activities of a non-profit

6

educational institution. in a classroom or similar place devoted to instruction, unless, in the case of a motion picture or other audio visual work, the performance, or display of individual images, is given by means of a copy that was not lawfully made under this title, and that the person responsible for the performance knew or had reason to believe was not lawfully made.   #17 USC Section 110(1)

b. Transmission of Audio Visual Materials: By definition, transmission of AV materials to classrooms, homes or work sites constitutes public performances and requires appropriate licenses. Educational institutions have special exemptions allowing transmission of performances of a nondramatic literary or musical work or display of a work, by or in the course of a transmission if-
        a. the performance or display is a regular part of the systematic instructional activities of a governmental body or a nonprofit educational institution; and
        b. the performance or display is directly related and of material assistance to the teaching content of the transmission; and
        c. the transmission is made primarily for-
        (I)reception in classroom or similar places normally devoted to instruction....   #17 USC Section 110(2)

NOTE: The above does not apply to the performance of dramatic literary or musical works nor does it permit transmission of motion pictures or other audio visual works. To comply with copyright, at the time of purchase or rental, the Division's purchase orders include a statement indicating that the material(s) may be used on the campus closed circuit system. Materials from vendors who refuse to grant this right are marked to be carted to the classrooms.

3. Off-Air Videotaping

In 1981, a negotiating committee made up of representatives of education organizations, creative guilds and unions, and copyright proprietors published guidelines for the application of Fair Use to the recording, retention, and use of television broadcast programs for education use.

1. The guidelines were developed to apply only to off-air recording by nonprofit educational institutions.
2. A broadcast program may be recorded off-air simultaneously with broadcast transmission (including simultaneous cable retransmission) and retained by a nonprofit educational institution for a period not to exceed the first forty-five (45) consecutive calendar days after date of recording. Upon conclusion of such retention period, all off-air recordings must be erased or

7

destroyed immediately. "Broadcast programs" are television programs transmitted by television stations for reception by the general public without charge.

3. Off-air recordings may be used once by individual teachers in the course of relevant teaching activities, and repeated once only when instructional reinforcement is necessary, in classrooms and similar places devoted to instruction within a single building, cluster or campus, as well as in he homes of students receiving formalized home instructions, during the first ten (10) consecutive school days in the forty-five 945) day calendar day retention period. "School days" are school session days - not counting weekends, holidays, vacations, examination periods, and other scheduled interruptions-within the forty-five (45) calendar day retention period.

4. Off-air recordings may be made only at the request of and used by individual teachers, and may not be regularly recorded in anticipation of requests. No broadcast program may be recorded off-air more than once at the request of the same teacher, regardless of the number of times the program may be broadcast.

5. A limited number of copies may be reproduced from each off-air recording to meet the legitimate needs of teachers under these guidelines. Each such additional copy shall be subject to all provisions governing the original recording.

6. After the first ten (10) consecutive school days, off-air recordings may be used up to the end of the forty-five (45) calendar day retention period only for teacher evaluation purposes i.e., to determine whether or not to include the broadcast program in the teaching curriculum, and may not be used in the recording institution for student exhibition or any other non-evaluation purpose without authorization.

7. Off-air recordings need not be used in their entirety, but the recorded programs may not be altered from their original content. Off-air recordings may not be physically or electronically combined or merged to constitute teaching anthologies or compilations.

8. All copies of off-air recording must include the copyright notice on the broadcast program as recorded.

9. Educational institutions are expected to establish appropriate control procedures to maintain the integrity of these guidelines. Guidelines For Off-air Recording of Broadcast Programming For Educational Purposes

4. Taping Television Programs Off Satellite

Satellite programming and transmission is governed by Title 47 of the U.S. Code, the Federal Communications Act, and falls under the jurisdiction of the Federal Communications Commission. Recording and/or distribution of satellite signals requires a license since Fair Use exemptions under the

8

copyright law do not apply.

5. Computer Software

In December, 1980, the copyright law was amended to include a definition of a computer program (#17 USC Section 101) and the statement that the owner of a copy of a computer program is not infringing copyright by making or authorizing the making of another copy or adaptation of the program provided:

a. that such a copy or adaptation is created as an essential step in the utilization of the computer program in conjunction with a machine and that it is used in no other manner, or

b. that such new copy or adaptation is for archival purposes only and that all archival copies are destroyed in the event that continued possession of the computer program should cease to be rightful.   #17 USC Section 117

Any copies prepared or adapted may not be sold or given away without the copyright holder's permission. Guidelines have been prepared by the International Council for Computers in Education but provide little information beyond restating the law.

6. Multimedia, Laser Discs, CD-ROMS, Computer Scanning, etc.

The law is silent or very sparse in the area of new technology. As with other mediums, a person may copy, prepare a derivative work, sell or lease, publicly perform or display only under certain exemptions in the law or Fair Use circumstances. The fact that it is possible to clip, sample, morph, resequence, merge and edit a wide variety of images into any format does not permit the capture and use of copyrighted material without permission of the author or purchase of a license.

LIBRARY APPLICATIONS

The Division strongly endorses the rights of authors, producers, and publishers as protected by the copyright law and rigorously supports the law. The Division's staff are prohibited from copying copyrighted works unless the action is authorized by specific exemptions in the copyright law, the principle of fair use, the fair use guidelines, licenses or written permission from the copyright owner. It is the responsibility of the librarians to ensure that all equipment and materials under their supervision are labeled with appropriate copyright warning notices as outlined in the law and that any records mandated by the law are maintained.

9

Library Photocopying:

1. Section 108 allows a library and its employees acting within the scope of their employment, to reproduce one copy or phonorecord of a work or to distribute such copy or phonorecord under the conditions below:

a. the reproduction or distribution is made without any purpose of direct or indirect commercial advantage

b. the collections of the library are (a) open to the public, or (b) available not only to researchers affiliated with the library or with the institution of which it is a part, but also to other persons doing research in a specialized field

c. the reproduction or distribution of the work includes a notice of copyright.   #17 USC Section 108(a)

2. Reproduce unpublished works for the purpose of preservation and security.   #17 USC Section 108(b)

3. Reproduce published works for the purpose of replacement of damaged, deteriorating, lost or stolen copies if replacements cannot be obtained at a fair price.   #17 USC Section 108(c)

4. Reproduce for a user one single copy of one article or small part of a work if-

a. the copy becomes the property of the user and the library has had no notice that the copy would be used for any purpose other than private study, scholarship or research; and

b. the library displays prominently at the place where orders are accepted, and includes on its order form, a warning of copyright.   #17 USC Section 108(d)

5. Reproduce an entire work at the request of a user if the library has first determined on the basis of a reasonable investigation that a copy cannot be obtained at a fair price, if:

a. the copy becomes the property of the user and the library has had no notice that the copy would be used for any purpose other than private study, scholarship or research; and

b. the library displays prominently at the place where orders are accepted, and includes on its order form, a warning of copyright.   #17 USC Section 108(e)

6. Nothing in this section:

a. shall be construed to impose liability for copyright infringement upon a library or its employees for the unsupervised use of reproducing equipment located on its premises provided that such equipment displays a notice that the making of a copy may be subject to the copyright law;

10

b. excuses a person who uses such equipment or who requests a copy under Section 108(d) from liability for copyright infringement or for any later use of the copy, if it exceeds fair use as provided by Section 107;

c. shall be construed to limit the reproduction of a limited number of copies and excerpts by a library of an audiovisual news program, subject to clauses (1), (2), and (3) of Section 108(a); or

d. affects the right of fair use as provided by Section 107 or any contractual obligations assumed at any time by the library when it obtained a copy or phonorecord of a work for its collections.   #17 USC section 108(f)

NOTE: All of the proceeding are for isolated and unrelated reproduction on difference occasions. Systematic, single reproduction is prohibited. Libraries and library employees are given notice in Section 108 (g)(1)(2) that the rights of reproduction do not extend to multiple copying of the same materials on one occasion or over a period of time, and intended for aggregate use by one or more individuals or for the separate use by individual members of a group.

e. rights of reproduction under this section do not apply to:

1. Musical works
2. Pictorial, graphic or sculptural works
3. Motion picture or other audiovisual works (except as outlined in Section 108(f)

Library Photocopying for Reserve Use: The Copyright Law does not specifically address copying for reserve use. Library photocopying for reserve use may be permissible if all of the four Fair Use criteria in Section 107 are met:

1. Purpose and character of Use
2. Nature of the work
3. Amount and substantiality of the portion used
4. Effect upon the potential market for the work.

The Division and the staff are responsible for carefully examining reserve requests, monitoring the number of copies made, keeping the quantities of copies to a minimum, ensuring that only small sections of a total work have been reproduced, and marking all copies with the copyright notice.

Library Photocopying for Interlibrary Loan: Section 108(g)(2) addresses interlibrary loan with a proviso that nothing in this clause prevents a library from participating in interlibrary arrangements if the library receiving the

11

copies or phonorecords does not do so in such aggregate quantities as to take the place of a subscription or purchase of materials. The National Commission on New Technological Uses of Copyrighted Works, a commission charged by Congress and representing principal library, author and publisher organizations, agreed to the following detailed guidelines which were accepted into the Conference Report of the 94th Congress.

1. Within a calendar year, a library may request no more than five copies of articles from a given title (as opposed to individual issues) during the five years preceding the request. These guidelines do not apply to any request for a copy or copies of an article or articles published in any issues of a periodical prior to the five year period.

2. Within any calendar year, a library is limited to a total of five copies of excerpts from a book or pamphlet during the time it is covered by copyright.

3. The above limitations do not apply if:
    a. the library has placed a subscription to the periodical
    b. the library owns the work but the copy is not reasonably available for copying, i.e. lost, checked out, stole or other wise unavailable
    c. the library has ordered the title but it has not arrived

Under these circumstances the library may request a copy under the guidelines in Section 108.

4. Requests made under these guidelines may not be filled unless the request is accompanied by a statement that the request does conform with these guidelines.

5. The requesting library shall maintain records of all requests made by it for copies of phonorecords of any materials to which these guidelines apply and shall maintain records of the fulfillment of such requests. These records shall be retained until the end of the third complete calendar year after the end of the calendar year in which the request was made.

Fax Copying: A fax machine is a copying machine and is subject to the same rules for classroom, library, and interlibrary loan photocopying . The necessity of making a photocopy of the material in order to use the fax machine is not a violation as long as the photocopy is destroyed after transmission. The law does not permit the library to keep a photocopy of an article, book, etc. and, in fact, subsections (d) and (e) specifically require that the copy become the property of the user.   #17 USC Section 108

Lending of Materials: Notwithstanding the provisions of Section 106(3), the owner of a particular copy or phonorecord lawfully made under this title, or any person authorized by such owner, is entitled, without the authority of the copyright owner, to sell or otherwise dispose of the possession of that copy or phonorecord.   #17 USC Section 109(a)

In addition:

   1. Section 109(b)(1)(A) permits the rental, lease or lending of a phonorecord for nonprofit purposes by a nonprofit library or nonprofit educational institution. The transfer of possession of a lawfully made copy of a computer program by a nonprofit educational institution to another such institution or to faculty, staff, and students does not constitute rental, lease or lending for direct or indirect commercial purposes.   #17 USC Section 109

   2. Subsection (B) states that the above does not apply to a computer program embodied a machine or product which cannot be copied during ordinary operation or use of the machine or product.   #17 USC Section 109

   3. Subsection (b)(2)(A) states that nothing in Subsection (b) shall apply to the lending of a computer program for nonprofit purposes by a nonprofit library, if each copy of a computer program which is lent by such library has affixed to the packaging containing the program a warning of copyright in accordance with requirements that the Register of Copyrights shall prescribe by regulation.   #17 USC Section 109

Viewing of Materials: As with printed materials, when the division purchases videotapes and other audio visual materials, it purchases the physical object as distinct from purchasing the copyright therein. Copyright regulations determine what the division can and cannot do with materials it purchases without infringing upon the copyright it does not own.

   1. The law does not grant libraries public performance exemptions but because a library may be "a similar place devoted to instruction," the classroom exemption in Section 110(1) protects the public showing of videotapes in the library where the requirements of that section are met. Generally works that are viewed privately by an individual library user is a private performance and does not infringe the copyright holder's rights. For instance, a musical recording or videotape checked out by a user and played in a carrel or viewing room is not a public performance. Works performed for a very small group may not be a public performance but the size of the group is a critical factor.

   2. If the viewing of materials by a large group of persons does not fall under

13

Section 110(1). performance rights or licenses are required. As a rule. libraries which purchase copyrighted motion pictures do not receive performance rights. These rights must be purchased separately. The Division of Library Services does not purchase and does not have public performance rights to the materials in its audio visual collection.

3. Videotapes rented from a retail video store may not be used by a library for public performance since they are intended for home use only. There is some confusion about whether purchased copies of video tapes that carry a home use only warning may be performed in a library in a nonprofit institution. The American Library Association takes the position that students may view in the library as part of instruction videotapes with a home use warning. The Media Producers Association, the Motion Picture Association of America and other copyright holders disagree with ALA's interpretation.

The statement below has been prepared by a vendor and reviewed for accuracy by the Motion Picture Association of America:

> *The copyright law is very clear in permitting the showing of motion pictures and other audiovisual materials in a classroom within a non-profit educational institution as long as it is part of "face-to-face" teaching activities. The use must be part of the instructional program and cannot by shown for recreation or entertainment. Section 110(1) of the Copyright Law exempts the classroom use of a lawfully manufactured and obtained copy of a motion picture from the public performance rights reserved to the copyright holder. This section of the law states:*
>
> > *Notwithstanding the provisions of Section 106, the following are not infringements of copyright:*
> >
> > *1) performance or display of a work by instructors or pupils in the course of face-to-face teaching activities of a non-profit educational institutions in a classroom or similar place devoted to instruction, unless in the case of a motion picture or other audiovisual work, the performance, or display of individual images, is given by means of a copy that was not lawfully made under this title, and that the person responsible for the performance knew or had reason to believe was not lawfully made.*
>
> *With respect to where a motion picture or videocassette may be shown, the term "classroom or similar place" is defined on page 82 of House Hearing report 94-1476 to mean a place which is devoted to instruction and would include a studio, a workshop, a gymnasium. a training field, a library, the stage of an auditorium, or the auditorium itself, if actually used as a classroom for systematic instructional activities.*
>
> *It should also be noted that any duplication or copying of a videocassette is illegal. This would apply even to the making of an archival copy or transferring from one format to another.*
>
> *Statement prepared by Social Studies School Service and reflects suggestions by the Motion Picture Association of America after its review. The statement was approved by*

14

the Association for Education Communications & Technology and was reprinted in its January/February, 1984 newsletter, Access.

OBTAINING PERMISSION

For permission to copy materials that do not meet the exceptions in Sections 107 and 108 (or any other exceptions to the copyright holder's exclusive rights), the user must contact the copyright holder or a licensing agency prior to copying the material.

When requesting permission from a copyright holder, it is important to recognize that the law does not require the holder to grant permission for the proposed use. The owner has the right to deny permission and a user denied permission has no legal recourse.   If the copyright holder grants permission (with or without conditions), the owner does so as a matter of choice, not legal obligation.

The Association of American Publishers has determined that the following facts are necessary to authorize duplication of copyrighted materials:

1. Title, author and/or editor, and edition of materials to be duplicated
2. Exact material to be used, giving amount, page numbers, chapters and, if possible, a photocopy of the material
3. Number of copies to be made
4. Use to be made of duplicated materials
5. Form of distribution
6. Whether or not the material is sold
7. Type of reprint (ditto, photocopy, offset, typeset)

Two copies of the request (one to be mailed back and one for the owner's files) should be sent with a self-addressed return envelope to the permissions department of the publisher in question.   The request should include spaces at the bottom of the letter for the owner's approval, including signature, date and conditions (if any).

The Division maintains files of all requests for permission to duplicate materials issued from the Director's office. In addition, this office maintains a file of forms, letters, etc. outlining restrictions on use received at the time of purchase.

Sample letters are attached in Appendix A..

CONCLUSION

For the most part, all of the printed, audio visual and computer materials that are

15

part of the library's collections are copyrighted with the bundle of rights which make up a copyright belonging to the copyright holder. Under the first sale doctrine, a purchaser may do many things with materials s/he acquires including lending, renting and giving them away. The making of copies and the adapting and performing of materials, however, are not privileges accorded to the purchaser. To increase the public's access to information, libraries were granted some specific rights as well as limited means for use of materials under the fair use doctrine .

Beyond this, two simple facts underlie copyright. First, you may do with copyrighted material anything you like IF you can obtain permission in writing from the holder of the copyright. Getting permission takes planning and time, but copyright holders are generally willing to give permission if you make a reasonable request for the use of their material. Second, it is possible to pay through licenses and other fees for the right to use copyrighted materials. Such agencies as the Copyright Clearance Center have been established to collect money for copyright holders whose materials are copied on a regular basis. When these facts are coupled with the rights granted to scholars and educational institutions under the law, little excuse exists for infringements to occur.

Unfortunately, a number of authors have noted that there is a widespread attitude that no one would sue a library over copyright. This is simply not true. It is not necessary for an infringement suit to go to court for the violator to be liable for monetary penalties. In fact suits are often settled out of court for relatively small amounts of money but the time, effort and stress caused by such a suit are incalculable not to mention the embarrassment of being caught infringing on the rights and creativity of scholars, publishers, and producers whom libraries generally support.

The Division has taken the position that the best practice is to be familiar with the copyright law, diligent in keeping current on changes, and err on the side of caution. This document is one effort it has made to inform the staff of the library applications of the copyright law. Since the copyright law is constantly being defined in court, a document such as this is soon out of date. Professional journals devoted to library and education often have columns devoted to copyright issues or contain news and articles on important developments concerning copyright. As the Division becomes aware of reinterpretations and definitions through court cases, supplements will be prepared to keep the information current.

7/6/95
S:\LIBADM\MANUAL\COPYRIGH.94

16

Tallahassee Community College

BIBLIOGRAPHY

Bielefield, Arlene and Lawrence Cheeseman. Libraries & Copyright Law. KF/3030.1/.B53/1993

Becker, Gary H. Copyright: A Guide to Information and Resources. 1992 Uncataloged

Blumenstyk, Goldie. "Publishers Win Ruling on Copyright." The Chronicle of Higher Education. November 9, 1994. A8

Copyright Law of the United States of America Contained in Title 17 of the United States Code. Revised to February 1, 1993. Uncataloged

Fair Use of Copyrighted Works. Report to Accompany H.R. 4412, House of Representatives. 102D Congress, 2d Session.   Uncataloged

Dukelow, Ruth. The Library Copyright Guide. KF/2989.5/D85/1992

Loving, Bill. A Multitude of risks in Multimedia. 1993. Uncataloged.

Miller, Jerome. Applying the New Copyright Law: A Guide for Educators and Librarians. KF/2995/.M54

Miller, Jerome and others. Video Copyright Permissions: A Guide to Securing Permission to Retain, Perform, and transmit Television Programs Videotaped Off The Air. KF/3030.4/.V53/1989

Morgan, Rebecca. "Getting Copyright Permission." Supervision, May, 1995, p. 9

Mullin, Bill. "Copyrights on the New Frontier". Tech Trends, January/February, 1994, pp. 14-15

The Official Fair-use Guidelines. 4th edition. 1989. REF/KF/2996/.O334/1989

Patry, William F. Copyright Law and Practice. Volumes 1-3. 1994. Uncataloged

Reed, Mary H. The Copyright Primer for Librarians and Educators. Z/649/.F35/H44/1987

Questions and Answers on Copyright for the Campus Community. 1989. Uncataloged

Reproduction of Copyrighted Works by Educators and Librarians. Circular 21.
    Copyright Office. 1992. Uncataloged

Steinhilber, August. Copyright Law: A Guide for Public Schools.
KF/2994/.S731/1986

Talab, Rosemary S. "Copyright and Other Legal Considerations in Patron-use
    Software." Library Trends. No. 1, Summer, 1991, pp. 85-96

_____ "Copyright, Legal, and Ethical Issues in the Internet
Environment." Tech Trends. March, 1994, pp. 12-14

 A Viewer's Guide to Copyright Law: What Every School, College and Public
Library Should Know. 1992. Uncataloged

Vleek, Charles W. Adoptable Copyright Policy. KF/1994/.V56/1992

Wright, A. J. Copyright in Cyberspace: Intellectual Property and Electronic
Media and Networks. 1993. Uncataloged

COPYRIGHT

© POLICIES & INFORMATION

❋ PimaCommunityCollege

Where can I get further Information on Copyright?

As already noted, the *Guidelines for Educators* document is available in campus libraries and in most administrative offices. The college also has established a Copyright Committee. Each committee member is responsible for serving specific locations in the college, and each has a supply of "Copyright Permission Request Forms" and "Media Permission Request Forms." Your campus/locational representative will be happy to assist you if you need to request permission to reprint or duplicate materials. Committee members can also field questions about copyright which may not be specifically addressed in this brochure or in the larger guidelines document. Committee members are noted on the organization chart.

Copyright Committee Organization

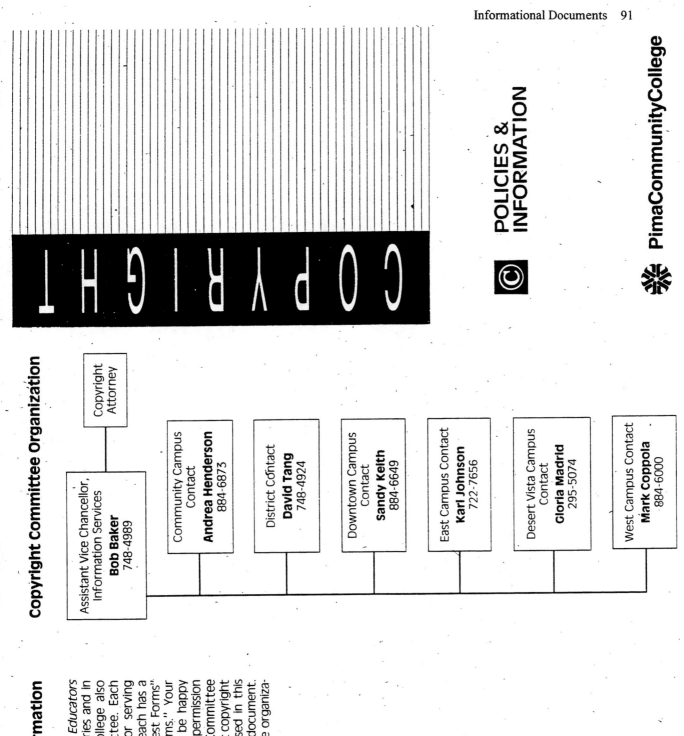

Copyright Attorney

Assistant Vice Chancellor, Information Services
Bob Baker
748-4989

Community Campus Contact
Andrea Henderson
884-6873

District Contact
David Tang
748-4924

Downtown Campus Contact
Sandy Keith
884-6649

East Campus Contact
Karl Johnson
722-7656

Desert Vista Campus Contact
Gloria Madrid
295-5074

West Campus Contact
Mark Coppola
884-6000

Pima County Community College

Some Information on Copyright

The Board of Governors of Pima Community College has adopted a policy which calls for all college employees — faculty, staff, and administrators — to be familiar with and abide by the provisions of the federal copyright law. The policy, adopted by the Board of Governors at its January 1991 meeting, reads as follows:

Pima County Community College District and its employees will adhere to current U.S. Copyright Law. Employees are prohibited from copying materials not specifically allowed by the Copyright Law: Fair Use Guidelines; Licenses or contractual agreements; or express permission from the copyright holder.

The purpose of this brochure is to share some basic information about that law and its provisions so that as a PCC employee you are familiar with what you are allowed to copy and what you are not allowed to copy. A more detailed document on copyright – *Guidelines for Educators* – is available in each of the campus libraries as well as in most administrative offices. Also, those areas of the college which are responsible for duplication of both print or non-print materials will also have reference copies available for consultation.

What is the Copyright Law?

The Copyright Law of the United States (Title 17, U.S. Code) protects "original works of authorship" regardless of the medium of expression. It thus covers the rights to make copies of books, periodicals, videotapes, films, sound recordings, and computer software (to name but a few). Although the primary purpose of the law is to provide protection for authors' interests in their own "intellectual property," the law also acknowledges the legitimate "fair use" of intellectual property.

What are the penalties for infringement?

Penalties for infringement of copyright can range from $500 to $20,000 per occurrence, although courts can increase the damages to $100,000 if the infringement was deemed to be "willful." However, no statutory damages can be assessed against an employee of an educational institution who, while acting within the scope of his or her duties, can prove that he or she had reasonable grounds for believing that his use of copyrighted material in question was a "fair use."

What is "Fair Use"?

When the Copyright Law was revised in 1976, the Congress specifically indicated that non-profit educational institutions could be allowed to use copyrighted materials in the following circumstances:

- Teachers can make a single copy of (a) a chapter of a book; (b) an article from a periodical or newspaper; (c) a short story, short essay or short poem; (d) a chart, diagram, cartoon or picture from a book, periodical or newspaper. The single copy can be made by or for a teacher for his or her own use for teaching, research, or class preparation.

- Multiple copies for classroom use (not to exceed the number of students in the class) may be made by or for a teacher so long as the copies are brief, the use is spontaneous, the copying is for one course only, and the copying is not intended to create or replace or substitute for an anthology. Also the multiple copies cannot be from a "consumable" workbook, and the copying cannot be repeated from term to term. Note that the "Fair Use Guidelines" actually specify in great detail what constitutes "brief" and "spontaneous." Information about these definitions is contained in the longer and more detailed *Guidelines for Educators* document mentioned above.

- There are separate guidelines for the "fair use" of music, audiovisual works, television programs, and some other materials. There are also some specific guidelines for the copying of copyrighted print and non-print materials in libraries. These guidelines are also outlined in more detail in the *Guidelines for Educators* document.

The description of "fair use" here is meant to be suggestive only. If you find that you need to make copies of copyrighted material, you should take the time to consult the more detailed *Guidelines* document.

Is computer software covered by the Copyright Law?

Yes it is. Thus, unless specifically stated otherwise on the license agreement that accompanies most commercially produced software, you cannot borrow or lend computer software from one college microcomputer to another. Most computer software license agreements indicate that you are allowed to make a single "backup" copy for archival purposes only.

(continued)

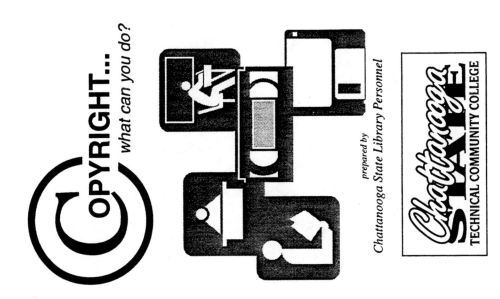

Copyright...
what can you do?

prepared by
Chattanooga State Library Personnel

Chattanooga STATE
TECHNICAL COMMUNITY COLLEGE

Chattanooga State Technical Community College is an equal opportunity institution.
Pub. No. 11-70-40000-1-8/93 BAPmktg

Multiple Copies for Classroom Use

All copying in an educational setting is based on the "Fair Use" clause in Section 107 of the U.S. Copyright Act of 1976. This clause allows for multiple copies for classroom use provided that this copying meets its criteria for spontaneity, brevity and cumulative effect. These criteria are:

- **Brevity:** a complete poem if less that 250 words or an excerpt of not more that 250 words; a complete prose work of less than 2,500 words or an excerpt of not more that 1,000 words or 10% of the work, whichever is less, but a minimum of 500 words;

- **Spontaneity:** the copying is at the inspiration of the individual teacher and the decision to use the work is such that it is unreasonable to expect a timely reply to a request for permission;

- **Cumulative Effect:** the copying is for only one course in the school in which the copies are made; not more than one short poem or prose work or more than two excerpts may be copied from the same author nor more than three copies from the same collective work or periodical volume during one class term; and there should be no more than nine instances of such multiple copying for one course during one class term.

The instructor is prohibited from:

- copying to replace or substitute for published anthologies;

- copying consumable materials such as workbooks, exercises, standardized tests, test booklets, and answer sheets;

- copying to substitute for the purchase of books, periodicals, or reprints; and

- charging the student beyond the actual cost of photocopying.

Should the instructor wish to create his own anthology for use in the classroom, he should see the College Bookstore manager who can refer him to a legal custom publishing company called Custom Academic Publishing Company. This company can secure all the necessary copyright clearances, pay appropriate royalties, print, and bind the document.

Conclusion

A copy of all guidelines and copyright information mentioned in this brochure is on reserve in the Library. Copyright infringements place the instructor and the institution at risk. Two types of damages are assessed against the institution: actual damages and profits, and statutory damages. Statutory damages range from $200 per instance for innocent infringement to $100,000.00 per instance for willful infringement. Careful planning by the instructor and an awareness of the instructor's rights under the "Fair Use" clause should prevent any instances of copyright infringement.

What Can You Do?

This information on copyright is provided to you by the Chattanooga State Library in order to increase your awareness of the importance of copyright compliance in a college setting. Copyright concerns continually confront the instructor as he plans course content. Special concerns include library reserves, videotapes, computer software, interlibrary loans, and multiple copies for classroom use. This brochure attempts to answer some of the more common dilemmas facing the instructor in dealing with copyright.

Library Reserves

The instructor may place the original, library-owned work on reserve for as long as necessary, but a photocopy of the same work or excerpt of the work must adhere to the following guidelines:

- the material includes a copyright notice on the first page of the portion photocopied;
- the number of copies should be in proportion to the number of students using the material, and the number of other courses that may assign the same material;
- the effect of photocopying the material should not be detrimental to the market for the work;
- consumable materials, such as workbooks, cannot be copied or put on reserve as that would be detrimental to the market for the work.
- photocopies of printed material may be put on reserve for one semester unless purchased by the library or through an authorized document delivery service which provides for payment of copyright fees.

Videotapes

All videotapes owned by Chattanooga State Library have been legally purchased and licensed for broadcasting over the closed circuit and ITFS. Under the copyright law and in compliance with our licensing agreements, Chattanooga State **cannot** make multiple copies of videotapes or lend the videotapes to other institutions or interested parties unless permission to do so was granted in the original licensing agreement. The institution may go back to the copyright holder and ask for these permissions, but that takes time and requires prior planning on the part of the instructor needing extra tapes. Chattanooga State follows the Videotaping Guidelines for Off-air Recording by Non-Profit Educational Institutions. Any TV program (except HBO, SHOWTIME, etc.) can be recorded and retained for 45 days. It may be used in a classroom setting for the first 10 days only and retained for 35 days for purposes of evaluation and for the purpose of negotiating a license for retention.

Videotapes for home use only may not be shown over the closed circuit or ITFS without first being licensed for such use by the college.

For more information about videotapes in the college setting please refer to the TBR brochure "Video, Copyright & the College Professor."

Computer Software

Unless specifically prohibited, the owner of a computer program may make one copy or adaptation of the program in three instances:

- for archival purposes in order to guard against damage from mechanical failure;
- as a necessary step to use the program with a machine (i.e., to convert from 5 1/4" to 3 1/2" diskette);
- to add features to the program for personal use only.

Interlibrary Loans

An instructor may request for his own personal use magazine articles from magazines not owned by this institution. The mechanism for making these requests is through the Interlibrary Loan Service provided by the Library. The Library adheres to the Interlibrary Loan Guidelines of the American Library Association.

Without paying copyright fees, the Library may borrow as many as five articles per year from a periodical title going back five years and as many articles as the instructor needs from periodical titles going back more than five years. If the Library has a current subscription to the periodical, it may request as many articles as needed.

Manatee
Community
College

Campus Information
Copyright Guidelines
1996 - 1997

23

Computer Software

When you purchase a software package, the copyright holder (publisher) of that package normally retains ownership of the software and grants you a license to use that software under certain restrictive conditions. Unless specifically stated otherwise on the license agreement of the package you have purchased, the following restrictions apply on all software purchased for use on MCC Personal Computers.

You may:
- Make a copy of the original diskettes, for **backup** purposes only.
- Use the software on only one machine at a time.
- Give or sell the package to another person or department, **provided** that they receive **all** the original written materials and diskettes, as well as any backup copies which you may have.

You may not:
- Install the product on more than one machine at a time.
- Make or allow diskette copies of the product to be distributed to other people or departments.
- Make copies of the documentation manuals (see note).
- Alter, modify, or adapt the software in any way without the copyright holder's written consent.

Note: Some software packages sell site licensing packages allowing a specific number of installations for a single price. A site license normally provides only one set of software diskettes and one set of documentation. Software and manuals may be copied to provide for one complete set for each software installation as outlined in the license agreement. **Each** installation of the software package is subject to all the rules above.

Failure to follow the above policy may result in disciplinary action, a civil suit, fines up to $100,000 and possible imprisonment.

Multimedia Productions

All copying, digitizing, or scanning of copyrighted materials to incorporate into your multimedia presentation (e.g. Powerpoint, Tool Book, dtc.) is covered by Copyright Law. Although specific guidelines are still being developed, when multimedia is created for educational purposes "Fair Use" Law applies. Before including copyrighted materials in your production, consider the amount and substantiality of the part used, compared to the work as a whole. (A single image or very small portion stands a greater chance of being considered "Fair Use.")

Whenever possible use clip art, licensed sound/video libraries, and/or original graphics, which are all available through Media Services in the Library. If in doubt whether use of a work is allowable under the law, request permission from the copyright owner(s); it's always the safest course of action.

Music

Copyrighted music may not be copied or performed without permission of the copyright owner. The provisions for "Fair Use" of copyrighted music by non-profit educational institutions for instructional use are listed below. All photocopies of music must display a copyright notice.

You may:
- Make emergency copies to replace purchased copies when the purchased copies are not available for an imminent performance. The purchased copies must be substituted for the emergency photocopies as soon as they are available.
- Make multiple copies of excerpts, representing no more than ten percent of the work, for academic purposes. The copy cannot constitute a performable unit.
- Make a single copy of an entire, performable unit, for academic purposes, if the work is confirmed to be out of print, and is not available in a larger work.
- Edit or simplify printed copies if the fundamental character of the work is not distorted or the lyrics altered.
- Make a single copy of a sound recording, owned by an educational institution, or an individual teacher, for aural exercises or examinations.
- Perform a work in face-to-face teaching activities. This does not extend to the performance of copies of works that have not been legally made.

Campus Information
Copyright Guidelines
1996 - 1997

24

Manatee
Community
College

Print Materials
Ordinarily you may not photocopy materials that are protected by copyright law without permission of the copyright owner. "Fair Use" laws outline exceptions under which copies may be made for use by an instructor of a non-profit educational institution for use in teaching, research, or scholarship. Additional guidelines specify the conditions under which copies may be made for classroom and reserve room use.

You may:
- Make a single copy of a book chapter, journal article, short story, essay, short poem; or a chart, graph, diagram, drawing, cartoon, or picture from a book, journal, or newspaper for research or teaching preparation.
- Make multiple copies of a journal article, book chapter, short story, essay, or poem for classroom or reserve room use, if

  - the article, chapter, story, or essay does not exceed 2500 words or the poem does not exceed 250 words.
  - the decision to use the copyrighted material for a particular class is spontaneous, and would not allow time to obtain permission from the copyright owner.
  - the copies are made for only one course in the college.
  - there are no more than two excerpts from one author.
  - there are no more than three copies made from the same book or journal volume during one semester.
  - there are no more than nine instances of multiple copying for one course during one semester.

You may not:
- Make copies to replace or substitute for anthologies, compilations, or collections of readings.
- Make copies from consumable works, such as workbooks, exercises, or standardized tests.
- Make or use copies from the same copyrighted material from semester to semester.
- Have copies made of copyrighted material at any commercial copy shops.

Audiovisual Materials
Copyright protects the format in which a producer expresses an idea, since ideas themselves are not protected. Therefore, making copies or changes from one format to another are NOT permitted. The following applies to educational use of copyrighted audiovisual materials, unless permission has been obtained to do otherwise.

You may:
- Request a program be recorded off-air if you show it within 10 school days of the original broadcast and erase it within 45 calendar days. This applies only for regular broadcast television, not for subscription/cable television.
- Tape it at home, although the 10 and 45 day rule still applies.
- Show the off-air tape in several classes, within the 10 school day period.
- Make multiple copies of locally produced, non-copyrighted materials.
- Show a video tape in class that was purchased or rented from a video store.
- Make a single slide or transparency from a book.

You may not:
- Record any subscription/cable programming for later use.
- Make duplicates of audio or video tapes.
- Use programming recorded from broadcast television in the classroom, if it is more than 10 school days old.
- Transfer one format to another, such as from 3/4" to 1/2" video, from film to video, or from paper to multiple slide/transparency sets.
- Edit or combine off-air recordings to create an anthology or new work.
- Make duplicates of slide sets.
- Use college equipment to show an illegally copied video tape.
- Use copyrighted music as part of a video or multimedia production.
- Instruct someone else to make illegal copies for you.

For More Information:
The above sections summarize when permission is not required to make reproductions. A good general rule is that any quote, excerpt, or other use of copyrighted material should be acknowledged and credited. (However, acknowledgement does not make copyright violations legal.)

If a question exists or exceptions to the above are desired, permission should be obtained. For more information on how to request it, check the more detailed copyright section in the appendix of the Faculty Handbook. For other information or answers to specific questions please call Paula Biles, ext. 4398.

SPECIFIC APPLICATIONS

Interlibrary Loan
Chattanooga State Technical Community College
Cottey College
Broome Community College

Library Reserves
Cottey College
Broome Community College

Print Duplication and Course Packets
University of Toledo
Pima County Community College
Broome Community College
Hillsborough Community College

Video Applications
Hillsborough Community College
North Country Community College
Springfield Technical College

Media Adaptation and Production
William Rainey Harper College
Pima County Community College
Broome Community College

Distance Learning
University of Maine at Augusta
Northwest Michigan College

Music and Fair Use
Austin Community College

Computer Software and Fair Use
Austin Community College
Hillsborough Community College
Kirkwood Community College

Materials Developed by Employees
Pennsylvania College of Technology

Chattanooga State Technical Community College

Interlibrary Loan Service: Request	**PERIODICAL**

Please print clearly. Absence of information may delay filling your request.

Periodical Title _____

Article Author _____

Article Title _____

Volume _____ Number _____

Date _____ Pages _____

Source of Citation, please give specifics: *Index used, or location of citation if from a bibliography.*

_____

_____

Name _____

Social Security Number _____

Address _____

_____

Home phone number _____ Call between hours of _____

Work phone number _____ Call between hours of _____

Today's date _____ Need before date _____

  Check one:

  _____ Student (Limit 5 items per week per student)

  _____ Faculty

  _____ Staff

Request reviewed by _____ (staff initials)

Please sign reverse side to indicate you have read the copyright restrictions warning. Thank you.

Chattanooga State Technical Community College is a Tennessee Board of Regents institution and an Equal Opportunity/Affirmative Action college.
Pub. No. 11-70-40000-2-7/95-hc-form# 68-new

WARNING

Copyright Restrictions

The copyright Law of the United States (Title 17, United States Code) governs the making of photocopies or other reproductions of copyrighted material.

Under certain conditions specified in the law, libraries and archives are authorized to furnish a copy or other reproduction. One of these specified conditions is that the photocopy or reproductions is not to be "used for any purpose other than private study, scholarship, or research." If a user makes a request for, or later uses, a photocopy or reproduction for purposes in excess of "fair use," that user may be liable for copyright infringement.

This institution reserves the right to refuse to accept a copying order, if in its judgement, fulfillment of the order would involve violation of the copyright law.

Please sign below to indicate you have read and understand this statement. Thank you.

_____

Signature

Ross Library   **Cottey College**

Interlibrary Loan Request Form

BORROWER

Name _____

Residence Hall _____ Phone _____

Today's Date _____

Please allow 10 to 14 days

Date Needed _____ for the item to arrive.

Faculty Signature _____
    If a faculty member signs that this request is part of
    an assignment, the student is not charged any fees.

$1 $3   If this request is not part of a class assignment,
           please circle the amount of fee you are willing to
$5 $10   pay for this item.

Please use a separate form for each item requested.

PERIODICAL ARTICLE > Use other side of sheet. >>

BOOK - Print clearly, please

Title of Book _____

_____ Year Pub._____

Author _____

Optional: *Optional:*
ISBN _____   *Edition Needed*_____

PERIODICAL ARTICLE - Print clearly, please

Title of Article _____

_____

Author of Article _____

Full Title of Periodical _____

_____

Vol._____   Issue Number _____   Pages _____

Date of Periodical _____

WARNING CONCERNING COPYRIGHT RESTRICTIONS

RK-Feb/95

BCC
LEARNING RESOURCES CENTER

INTERLIBRARY LOAN WORKFORM

A BCC Library card is required for identification and must be presented at the time this request is submitted as well as when the material is picked up from the Circulation Desk.

LIBRARIAN: Please **CHECK** for completeness, **VERIFY** for accuracy, and **INITIAL**: _____

DATE: _____ DATE NEEDED: _____
(CHECK WITH LIBRARY EVERY FEW DAYS, WE MAY NOT BE ABLE TO CONTACT YOU)

PATRON: _____ STU: _____ FAC: _____ OTHER: _____

LIBRARY CARD #: _____ DEPT: _____ PHONE: _____

ADDRESS: _____

Check One: Book Request _____   Magazine Request _____

AUTHOR: _____

TITLE: (OF BOOK OR ARTICLE) _____

_____

NAME OF JNL OR MAGAZINE: _____

ISSN/ISBN: _____

VOL: _____ NO: _____ DATE: _____ PAGES: _____
(FILL IN IF JOURNAL OR MAGAZINE ARTICLE IS REQUESTED)

VERIFIED: (SOURCE, SUCH AS INDEX): _____

ITEM WILL BE USED FOR: COURSE: _____ PROFESSIONAL: _____ PERSONAL: _____

IF THERE IS A FEE FOR OBTAINING THIS ITEM, ARE YOU WILLING TO PAY IT? _____ IF SO, UP TO WHAT AMOUNT? _____

BROOME COMMUNITY COLLEGE   *BOX 1017 - BINGHAMTON, NY 13902*

Ross Library   Cottey College

LIBRARY RESERVE FORM

DESCRIPTION OF THE ITEM TO BE PLACED ON RESERVE

Monograph
    Author _____

        Title _____

        Call Number _____

Periodical
    Title _____

        Date _____ Vol. ____ Issue _____ Pages _____

Individual Article or Selection Assigned from the Work

        Author _____

        Title _____

*Date placed on reserve_____   *Date to be removed _____

*Type of item: ___Library copy
                ___Photocopy - According to copyright guidelines it
                    is acceptable to place a photocopy of an
                    article on reserve for <u>one term</u>.
                ___Personal copy - May we place an adhesive book
                    pocket on your personal copy?
                                        ___Yes   ___No

FACULTY MEMBER'S ACKNOWLEDGEMENT OF FAIR USE
    I understand that systematic reproduction of copyrighted
material is a violation of copyright law. My students will be
assigned to <u>study</u> this material, not to copy it.

*Signature _____ Telephone _____

*Course _____ E-mail _____

*Type of reserve: ___1 hour in the Library
                    ___video (3 hours outside the Library)
                    ___overnight outside the Library
                    ___other
                    Please specify: _____

*Minimum information needed when this form is attached to the item.

                                                    RK 12/95

LIBRARY RESERVE SHEET

RESERVE MATERIALS MUST COMPLY WITH COPYRIGHT REGULATIONS

INSTRUCTOR: _____ EXT:_____ OFFICE:_____

COURSE NUMBER:_____

PLEASE LIST OTHER INSTRUCTORS WHOSE CLASSES MAY ALSO USE THIS RESERVE MATERIAL(S):

_____

ANY SPECIAL INSTRUCTIONS?_____

DATE ON RESERVE:_____OFF RESERVE:_____

WHERE CAN WE RETURN MATERIAL(S)?_____

*(USE: RU - ROOM USE; O - OVERNIGHT; WK - 1 WEEK)

BARCODE	LIB./FAC.	COPIES/FORMAT	AUTHOR	TITLE	USE*

Your signature certifies that the above listed materials to be placed on reserve are not copyrighted or comply with federal copyright laws for LRC reserve use or permission has been granted.

_____ _____
Signature   Date

Circulation Staff Member Taking Request:

_____

Date:_____ Time:_____

24 HOURS ARE NEEDED TO PLACE MATERIALS ON RESERVE

Broome Community College
P.O. Box 1017
Binghamton, NY 13902

COPYRIGHT PERMISSION REQUEST FOR LIBRARY RESERVE

To: _____   From: _____

_____   Date: _____

_____

We hereby request permission to make copies of the following information in order to place it on reserve in the Learning Resources Center at Broome Community College.

Author or Editor: _____

Article or Chapter Title: _____

Periodical or Book Title: _____

For Periodical - Volume # _____ Issue date _____ Pages _____ ISSN _____

For Book - Copyright date _____ Pages _____ ISBN _____

Number of copies to be placed on reserve: _____

Time item will remain on reserve: _____

These copies will be used exclusively for educational purposes, with no direct or indirect commercial advantage, and will include notice of copyright.

Please indicate your permission below and return this form within two weeks from the above date. A return envelope is enclosed for your convenience.

☐ Permission granted.

☐ Permission granted with the following restrictions: _____

_____

☐ Permission denied. (If so, is there another means by which we can make this material available to a large number of students?)
   ☐ Alternate Source: _____

Name *(Typed)* _____   Position _____

Signature _____   Date _____
   Broome Community College

The University of Toledo

Toledo, Ohio 43606-3390

Learning Resource Center
Scott Park Campus

Director
(419) 530-3175
msuter@uoft02.utoledo.edu

(419) 530-3194 FAX

Date

Publisher Name _____

Publisher Address   Copyrights and Permissions Department

_____

_____

Permission is requested to reproduce without fee the material listed below:

(For anthologies, a photocopy of the copyright acknowledgment page is provided if available.)

Author/Editor _____ ( ) Book ( ) Periodical ( ) AV Media

Title/Edition/Vol. # _____

Title of Article, Chapter, Video, etc. _____

ISBN/ISSN _____Publisher/Copyright Owner _____

Copyright Date _____ Check if appropriate ( ) OP ( ) Out of Stock ( ) NYP

Exact materials (page nos., frames, slides) to be duplicated _____

Maximum number of copies to be made_____

This material will be used for the following class:

Course Name and Number _____

Semester/Year _____

Instructor Name _____

A self-addressed envelope and a copy of this letter for your files are enclosed for your convenience.

Sincerely,

Permission granted _____   _____
                                        Signature   Date

Conditions, if any   _____

_____

_____

University of Toledo

HOW TO REQUEST COPYRIGHT PERMISSIONS

Whether you request permissions yourself, or through a college store or copy service, these suggestions will speed the process. **PLEASE:**

1. **Request permission as soon as possible.** Earlier is better in the event your request cannot be granted and you need to substitute other materials. Publishers do not always control rights and need time to research the extent to which permission may be granted.

2. **Direct your request to the publisher's Copyrights and Permissions Department, not the author.** If publishers do not control the rights, they will inform you whom to contact.

3. **Include all of the following information in your request:**

> a. author's, editor's, translator's full name(s)
> b. title, edition and volume number of book, journal, video, slide set, film, computer or CD disk
> c. copyright date
> d. ISBN for books, ISSN for magazines and journals
> e. numbers of exact pages, figures, illustrations, frames, programs
> f. if you are requesting a chapter or more: both exact chapter(s) and exact page numbers
> g. number of copies to be made
> h. whether material will be used alone or combined with other photocopied materials
> i. name of college or university
> j. course name and number
> k. quarter(s) and year(s) in which material will be used
> l. instructor's full name

4. **Request permission whether or not works are in print.**

5. **Provide your complete address and name of a contact person and telephone number in case there are any questions.**

In many cases your college book store or library can assist you and/or provide appropriate forms. The booklet, Questions and Answers on Copyright for the Campus Community is available from the UT Print Shop.

CopyrightPermissionRequest
PimaCountyCommunityCollegeDistrict

Date of Request:

To (Publisher's Name and Address):

Dear Permissions Officer:

I would like permission to duplicate the following materials for instructional use in a non-profit educational institution. This material will not be sold or used for any purpose other than instructional use.

Bibliographic citation:

Materials to be duplicated:

Number of copies:

Audience and format for proposed distribution:

Date of first use:

Period of extended use:

Type of duplication:

If you have any questions about this request, please phone (520) _____ . Thank you for your prompt attention to this matter.

Sincerely,

(Requestor's Name): _____   (Requestor's College Location): _____

(Requestor's Department: _____

Instructions to publisher/producer: Please retain the yellow copy for your files, and return the completed white copy
to the following address: *Office of Policy & Library Technology*
Pima Community College
4905C East Broadway Boulevard
Tucson, Arizona 85709-1130
Fax: (520) 748-4990

Permission _____ granted _____ denied
Conditions, if any:

_____   _____
Signature

_____
Name

_____
Title

_____
Date

91031A   White: Publisher returns to PCC   Canary: Publisher's Copy   Pink: Copyright Contact   Goldenrod: Requester

Pima County Community College

The Campus Store
Faculty-Student Association
of Broome Community College, Inc.

Textbook Requisition & Approval For Photocopied Course Material

Semester: _____

Instructor(s): _____ Course #(s): _____

This form requests the publication of classroom materials by the BCC Campus Store. Materials will be packaged as requested and will be sold to BCC students from the regular textbook shelves.

We cannot promise that this material will be available for student purchase the first date of instruction if this material does not meet the semester deadline for submission of text requisitions.

In order to provide the most legible copies, we prefer to use the original material. In cases where the original material is not available, please provide the best possible copy.

Please fill out one (1) form for each title to be printed.

> Please fill in the following information as you would like to see it appear on the cover:
>
> Course # _____ Author: _____
>
> Title: _____ Ed/Yr: _____

Please check the appropriate selections for finished package:

☐ Copy on one side of page   ☐ Copy on both sides of page
☐ Follow copy instructions on individual pages ☐ Staple
☐ Comb binding   ☐ Three hole punched
☐ Two pocket folder   ☐ Three ring binder
☐ Laminated front & back cover   ☐ Royalty $ _____ per copy
☐ Heavy coverstock front & back   ☐ Add On $ _____ per copy
                                              ☐ Other

In addition, is there any copyrighted material contained in the master to be photocopied?   ☐ Yes   ☐ No

If you answered yes to the above question, the copyrighted material MUST be disclosed and the attached Copyright Infringement Release MUST be completed.

Before the BCC Campus Store will accept photocopied course material, the following approval must be obtained:

Approved by: _____   _____
                        (Department Chairperson)   *(Date)*

(Please keep a photocopy of this completed form for your files and return the original to the BCC Campus Store.)

Broome Community College   9/93

The Campus Store
Faculty-Student Association
of Broome Community College, Inc.

Copyright Infringement Release

Prior to acceptance of any photocopied copyrighted materials from faculty for resale to students, the faculty memb presenting the materials must supply the information requested below and sign and date the completed form.

I, _____ , a member of the faculty of Broome Community College ha

delivered to the BCC Campus Store a master entitled: _____

to be photocopied for resale to students in course # _____ which includes certa

photocopies of copyrighted material (entitled) (excerpted from) _____

_____

I certify that each of these photocopies contains a page on which a notice of the copyright appears.

IMPORTANT:
Have you obtained, from the publisher or copyright owner, permission to make multiple copies of the copyrighted materia you have requested this store to sell to your students?

☐ Yes   ☐ No

If yes, attach a copy of the permission document to this release.

If no, do you wish to have the BCC Campus Store secure permission and bill the cost to the Academic Department?

☐ Yes   ☐ No

I, _____ , a member of the faculty of Broome Community College, do here agree to hold harmless the Faculty-Student Association of Broome Community College Inc., its employees and agents, and indemnify it from any claim, liability, expenses, damages, or costs of any nature incurred in connection with a charge copyright infringement arising out of the sale of the copyrighted materials described above.

_____   _____
(Faculty Signature)   *(Date)*

_____   _____
(Chairperson Signature)   *(Date)*

Further, if it is necessary to pay royalties to copy this material it will be the decision of the Dean of your Division to authoriz the printing of this material. If permission is granted by the Dean, royalties will be added as a fee to each copy printed for resal

_____   _____
(Dean)   *(Date)*

(Please keep a photocopy of this completed form for your files and return the original to the BCC Campus Store.)

ADMINISTRATIVE PROCEDURES

Title: COPYRIGHT COMPLIANCE: IN-HOUSE PUBLICATION OF INSTRUCTIONAL MATERIALS	Identification: 3.509
	Page: 1 of 1
	Effective Date: September 15, 1992

| Authority: SBE 6A-14.0262; 6A-14.0247 FS 240.319 Title 17 U.S. Code Sect. 101, et seq. | Signature/Approval: |

PURPOSE

The purpose of this administrative procedure is to establish guidelines regarding copyright compliance for in-house publication of instructional materials.

PROCEDURES

Faculty members are required to comply with all copyright laws and guidelines. (See Administrative Rule On Copyright Law Compliance, 6HX-10-3.010) and are encouraged to confer with the Bookstore Manager on any duplication concerned.

A faculty member requesting that printed material be sold in the bookstore, or requesting a single handout of more than 10 pages, must follow Administrative Procedure 3.104, In-house Publication of Instructional Materials.

Requests for duplication of printed material of less than 10 pages should follow Administrative Procedure 3.504, Copyright Compliance: Photocopying of Books, Periodicals, and Music.

The Bookstore subscribes to the National Association of College Stores (NACS) Copyright Permissions Service. When the Bookstore Manager receives the completed and approved Request to Print Instructional Materials form, the Bookstore Manager will use the NACS service to determine the availability of permissions to make multiple copies of the requested items and to print, or to print and sell, the published materials.

If permissions cannot be secured, the Bookstore Manager will contact the faculty member.

Copies of all permissions will be kept in the Bookstore Manager's office.

ADMINISTRATIVE PROCEDURES

Title: COPYRIGHT COMPLIANCE: PHOTOCOPYING OF BOOKS, PERIODICALS AND MUSIC	Identification: 3.504
	Page: 1 of 5
	Effective Date: September 15, 1992
Authority: SBE 6A-14.0262; 6A-14.0247 FS 240.319 Title 17 U.S. Code Sect. 101, et seq.	Signature/Approval:

PURPOSE

The purpose of this administrative procedure is to establish procedural guidelines regarding the reproduction/duplication of copyrighted materials.

PROCEDURE

The College adheres to the provisions of the United States Copyright Law (Title 17, U.S. Code, Section 101, et. seq.) and the provisions found in Section 107, "Fair Use."

The following sections outline the official minimum guidelines (reprinted here), that relate to classroom copying in a non-for-profit educational institution with respect to books, periodicals, and music. Fair use guidelines for off-air videotaping are found in the Hillsborough Community College Administrative Procedure 3.503.

These guidelines refer to the spontaneous copying of small amounts of materials. Faculty are encouraged to confer with the Bookstore Manager on all requests in which spontaneity is not an issue. For example: If a faculty member wants to make 100 copies of a two-page article to hand out to all sections of a course, the faculty member should confer with the Bookstore Manager on copyright permission, if there is sufficient time to do so.

For in-house publications and handouts of more than 10 pages, refer to Administrative Procedure 3.104, In-house Publication of Instructional Materials.

1.   GUIDELINES FOR BOOKS AND PERIODICALS

A.   Single Copying for Teachers - A single copy may be made of any of the following by or for a teacher at his/her individual request for his/her scholarly research or use in teaching or preparation to teach a class:

   (1)   A chapter from a book;

   (2)   An article from a periodical or newspaper;

ADMINISTRATIVE PROCEDURES

(3)   A short story, short essay or short poem, whether or not from a collective work; or

(4)   A chart, graph, diagram, drawing, cartoon or picture from a book, periodical, or newspaper.

B.   Multiple Copies for Classroom Use - Multiple copies (not to exceed in any event more than one copy per pupil in a course) may be made by or for the teacher giving the course for classroom use or discussion, provided that:

(1)   The copying meets the test of brevity and spontaneity as defined below; and;

(2)   meets the cumulative effect test as defined below; and,

(3)   each copy includes a notice of copyright.

The term brevity is defined as follows:

(i)   Poetry: (a) A complete poem if less than 250 words and if printed on not more than two pages or, (b) from a longer poem, an except of not more than 250 words.

(ii)   Prose: (a) Either a complete article, story or essay of less than 2,500 words, or (b) an excerpt from any prose work of not more than 1,000 words or 10% of the work, whichever is less, but in any event a minimum of 500 words.

The numerical limits stated in "i" and "ii" above may be expanded to permit the completion of an unfinished line of a poem or of any unfinished prose paragraph.

(iii)   Illustration: One chart, graph, diagram, drawing, cartoon or picture per book or per periodical issue.

ADMINISTRATIVE PROCEDURES

Identification:	Page:	Effective Date:
3.504	3 of 5	September 15, 1992

(iv) "Special" works: Certain works in poetry, prose or in "poetic prose" which often combine language with illustrations and which are intended sometimes for children and other times for a more general audience, and fall short of 2,500 words in their entirety. Paragraph "ii" above notwithstanding such "special works" may not be reproduced in their entirety; however, an excerpt comprised of not more than two of the published pages of such special work and containing not more than 10% of the words found in the text thereof, may be reproduced.

Spontaneity

(i) The copying is at the instance and inspiration of the individual teacher, and

(ii) The inspiration and decision to use the work and the moment of its use for maximum teaching effectiveness are so close in time that it would be unreasonable to expect a timely reply to a request for permission.

Cumulative Effect

(i) the copying of the material is for only one course in the school in which the copies are made.

(ii) Not more than one short poem, article, story, essay or two excerpts may be copied from the same author, nor more than three from the same collective work or periodical volume during one class term.

(iii) There shall not be more than nine instances of such multiple copying for one course during one class term.

The limitation stated in "ii" and "iii" above shall not apply to current news periodicals and newspapers and current news sections of other periodicals.

C. Prohibitions as to I and II Above - Notwithstanding any of the above guidelines, the following shall be prohibited:

ADMINISTRATIVE PROCEDURES

Identification: 3.504	Page: 4 of 5	Effective Date: September 15, 1992

(1) Copying shall not be used to create or to replace or as a substitute for anthologies, compilations or collective works. Such replacement or substitution may occur whether copies of various works or excerpts therefrom are accumulated or reproduced and used separately.

(2) There should be no copying of or from works intended to be "consumable" in the course of study or of teaching. These include workbooks, exercises, standardized tests and test booklets and answer sheets and like consumable materials.

(3) Copying books and periodicals shall not:

    (a)   substitute for the purchase of books, publishers' reprints or periodicals;

    (b)   be directed by higher authority; or

    (c)   be repeated with respect to the same item by the same teacher from term to term.

(4) No charge shall be made to the student beyond the actual cost of the photocopying.

2. GUIDELINES FOR EDUCATIONAL USES OF MUSIC

A. Permissible Uses

(1) Emergency copying to replace purchased copies which for any reason are not available for an imminent performance provided purchased replacement copies shall be substituted in due course.

(2) For academic purposes other than performance, single or multiple copies of excerpts of works may be made, provided that the excerpts do not comprise a part of the whole which would constitute a performable unit such as a selection, movement or aria, but in no case more than 10% of the whole work. The number of copies shall not exceed one copy per pupil.

(3) Printed copies which have been purchased may be edited or simplified provided that the fundamental character of the work is not distorted or the lyrics, if any, altered or lyrics added if none exist.

ADMINISTRATIVE PROCEDURES

Identification:	Page:	Effective Date:
3.504	5 of 5	September 15, 1992

(4)   A single copy of recordings of performances by students may be made for evaluation or rehearsal purposes and may be retained by the educational institution or individual teacher.

(5)   A single copy of a sound recording (such as a tape, disc or cassette) of copyrighted music may be made from sound recordings owned by an educational institution or an individual teacher for the purposes of constructing aural exercises or examinations and my be retained by the educational institution or individual teacher. (This pertains only to the copyright of the music itself and not to any copyright which may exist in the sound recording.)

B.   Prohibitions

(1)   Copying to create or replace or substitute for anthologies, compilations or collective works.

(2)   Copying of or from works intended to be "consumable" in the course of study or of teaching such as workbooks exercises, standardized tests and answer sheets and like material.

(3)   Copying for the purpose of performance, except as in A (1) above.

(4)   Copying for the purpose of substituting for the purchase of music, except as in A(1) and A(2) above.

(5)   Copying without inclusion of the copyright notice which appears on the printed copy.

ADMINISTRATIVE PROCEDURES

Title:	Identification: 3.505
COPYRIGHT COMPLIANCE:	Page: 1 of 1
PERMISSION TO COPY/USE	Effective Date: June 16, 1994

Authority:	Signature/Approval:
SBE 6A-14.0262; 6A-14.0247	
FS 240.319	
Title 17 U.S. Code Sect. 101, et seq.	

PURPOSE

The purpose of this administrative procedure is to establish guidelines regarding the request to duplicate copyrighted materials.

PROCEDURE

1. The request to duplicate/use any copyrighted material for any reason is the responsibility of the College employee needing the duplicated material. However, copies of all requests and permissions to copy must be on file with the Associate Vice President of Learning Resources Services (who is the College's Copyright Officer), with the Bookstore Manager, or with the Campus LRC.

2. Copyright permission letters from institutions and companies should be typed on business stationary and signed by the administrator who is responsible for copyright matters for that institution or company.

3. Permission letters from individuals do not need letterhead and may be accepted in handwritten form.

4. The permission letter should clearly state the granted rights, i.e.: to show the video on a closed circuit system, to duplicate 5 copies of an audio tape at no cost, to duplicate 200 copies of a poem and retain for the life of the paper, etc.

5. Permissions from copyright services, like the NACS Copyright Permission Service, are acceptable and encouraged. (See Administrative Procedures 3.504 and 3.104.)

ADMINISTRATIVE PROCEDURES

Title: COPYRIGHT COMPLIANCE: SHOWING VIDEO PROGRAMS ON IN-CLASS AND IN-LAB EQUIPMENT	**Identification:** 3.507 **Page:** 1 of 3 **Effective Date:** June 16, 1994
Authority: SBE 6A-14.0262; 6A-14.0247 FS 240.319 Title 17 U.S. Code Sect. 101, et seq.	**Signature/Approval:** *[signature]*

PURPOSE

The purpose of this administrative procedure is to establish guidelines for showing video programs on equipment which is placed in classrooms and learning labs.

PROCEDURE

Video programs can be shown in classrooms through a closed circuit system provided that permission to do so has been given for the specific video programs. If no permission has been received and/or if no closed circuit system is available, the following procedure should be followed:

1. **CLASSROOMS**

    A. Faculty are not to use their own equipment.

    B. A video program may be used only if it meets the educational objectives of the course. A video program may be selected from the following sources:

        1. The LRC/Learning Lab Video Collection;

        2. The District Video Collection;

        3. Materials rented through Campus LRC/AV Services from an authorized source; or

        4. Materials with the "For Home Use Only" label that do not belong to Hillsborough Community College, provided the video meets the requirements of Administrative Procedure 3.506, Copyright Compliance: Video Programs with the "Home Use Only" Warning Label.

    C. If a faculty member wishes to show a video program in a classroom and the source is from 1, 2, or 3 above, he/she should complete a Campus Film/Video Request form and notify the AV Technician that an in-class viewing is required. If the source is from 4 above, then a Request for Video Equipment must be submitted to the Campus AV Services. (See Administrative Procedure 3.305, Audiovisual Services.)

Hillsborough Community College

ADMINISTRATIVE PROCEDURES

Identification: 3.507	Page: 2 of 3	Effective Date: June 16, 1994

2.   <u>LEARNING LABS</u>

A.   Learning Lab personnel are responsible for monitoring the use of all learning lab equipment.

B.   Only video tapes owned or rented by the College, or those video tapes for which written permission has been obtained, may be used in labs. A request to use these video tapes must be submitted to learning lab personnel.

C.   Faculty requests to place audio visual programs not owned or rented by the College into learning labs must be cleared by the Campus Librarian and the Copyright Officer. Such programs must meet all copyright compliance procedures and permission letters must be on file with the Campus Learning Lab.

ADMINISTRATIVE PROCEDURES

Identification: 3.507	Page: 3 of 3	Effective Date: June 16, 1994

 HILLSBOROUGH COMMUNITY COLLEGE
REQUEST FOR VIDEO EQUIPMENT

This form is primarily for copyright compliance; however, it also alerts the Audio Visual Technician of your need for video equipment when you are personally bringing in a video tape from outside the HCC collection.

_____
DATE

REQUESTOR_____ Telephone_____

Type of equipment needed:

    1/2" VCR & TV_____   3/4" VCR & TV_____

    Delivery Date_____ Time_____.

    Deliver to_____ Campus _____ Bldg/Room_____

    Please state the title of the tape to be used and the source

    Title _____

    Source_____

Note: If you are bringing a video tape from outside the HCC collection, you must follow the HCC Administrative Procedures on Copyright Compliance (3.503, 3.507 and 3.508).

_____   _____
Requestor's Signature   Date

Original-Campus AV; Canary-Requestor

1-5-016 (04/94)

Hillsborough Community College

ADMINISTRATIVE PROCEDURES

Title:	Identification: 3.502
COPYRIGHT COMPLIANCE:	Page: 1 of 1
FILMS AND VIDEOS	Effective Date: September 15, 1992

Authority:	Signature/Approval:
SBE 6A-14.0262; 6A-14.0247 FS 240.319 Title 17 U.S. Code Sect. 101, et seq.	*[signature]*

PURPOSE

The purpose of this administrative procedure is to establish guidelines regarding the use of films and videos (for 16mm theatrical films or "Home Use Only" videos, see administrative procedure 3.506).

PROCEDURE

1. Whenever possible the College will purchase films and videos from distributors, not home video stores. Purchases and licenses of films and videos from distributors may include public performance rights. HCC is specifically interested in permission to show video programs through a closed circuit system.

2. All purchase orders for video programs will include the following statement:

    "Price includes rights to show the video (s) on the college's closed circuit television system."

3. All College-owned films and videos are for educational and instructional use only, preferably within HCC classrooms.

4. No College-owned films and videos may be rented to other educational institutions. Films and videos may be loaned to other educational institutions as available per standard interlibrary loan practice.

5. If public performance rights have been secured to do so, the films and videos may be used for extra curricular activities and fund raisers, but no admission may be charged.

6. Each College-owned film and video received after July 1, 1992 will be labeled regarding what performance activities are allowed.

Hillsborough Community College

ADMINISTRATIVE PROCEDURES

Title: COPYRIGHT COMPLIANCE: VIDEO PROGRAMS WITH THE "HOME USE ONLY" WARNING LABEL	Identification: 3.506
	Page: 1 of 2
	Effective Date: September 15, 1992

Authority: SBE 6A-14.0262; 6A-14.0247 FS 240.319 Title 17 U.S. Code Sect. 101, et seq.	Signature/Approval:

PURPOSE

The purpose of this administrative procedure is to establish guidelines for the use of video programs with the "Home Use Only" warning label.

PROCEDURE

1. In accordance with the Federal Copyright Guidelines, a faculty member may use a pre-recorded video program purchased or rented by the faculty member from a home video outlet, without the public performance license that is normally required. Each of the following guidelines must be met:

    A. The use must take place at Hillsborough Community College;

    B. The use must occur in a classroom or similar place devoted to instruction;

    C. The use must be part of the regular instructional process (not extra curricular or recreational);

    D. The use must be by the teacher and students (the teacher, students and video must all be face-to-face with no transmissions from outside of the building); and

    E. The video must be a lawfully made copy or the person responsible for the performance must have no reason to believe it is not a lawfully made copy. [Note: A copy taped at home is not "lawfully made" for use outside the home.]

2. Faculty who want to rent a video program bearing the "For Home Use Only" warning notice may rent the program at their own expense for use in their classroom, if the video meets all the criteria listed in #1 above. These rentals will not give permission for showing through a closed circuit system. Faculty will be required to request the appropriate equipment from the campus AV services (see Administrative Procedure 3.507).

ADMINISTRATIVE PROCEDURES

Identification:	Page:	Effective Date:
3.506	2 of 2	September 15, 1992

3.   The College may purchase or rent video programs with the warning label. When used, such programs must meet the criteria listed in #1 above and may be shown through the closed circuit system only with permission. (See Administrative Procedure 3.502, Copyright Compliance: Educational Films and Videos).

4.   A video program with the "Home Use Video Only" warning label, which is either purchased or rented by the College or by a faculty member, may not be used for any other purpose except planned, direct, instructional activities which meet course objectives, and the program must be used in a classroom, in face-to-face instruction. Permission to use on the closed circuit system must be noted on the video and the appropriate documentation must be on file. These videos may not be used for entertainment, funds raisers, or time fillers. Another use, other than institutional, will require a license agreement at the time of rental or purchase. In addition, any duplication or any form of copying of video programs is illegal and prohibited.

ADMINISTRATIVE PROCEDURES

Title: COPYRIGHT COMPLIANCE:	Identification: 3.503
OFF-AIR RECORDING OF BROADCAST TELEVISION	Page: 1 of 4
PROGRAMS FOR INSTRUCTIONAL USE	Effective Date: September 15, 1992

Authority:	Signature/Approval:
SBE 6A-14.0262; 6A-14.0247	
FS 240.319	*(signature)*
Title 17 U.S. Code Sect. 101, et seq.	

PURPOSE

The purpose of this administrative procedure is to establish procedural guidelines for off-air recording of broadcast television programs for instructional use.

PROCEDURE

Federal Copyright Guidelines permit the College to tape programs "off-air". Furthermore, the College is expected "to establish appropriate control procedures to maintain the integrity" of the guidelines. Hillsborough Community College has adopted the following published guidelines and has established controls as required by the Guidelines.

1. "Off-air taping" - refers only to open broadcast stations, or simultaneous cable retransmission. This means that a program can only be taped if it is coming over the airways. It does <u>not</u> include cable transmissions, except when they are simultaneous with the open broadcast.

    Examples: 1)   You receive a Chicago station on cable, but you could also receive it over the airways with an antenna.

    2)   You receive a premium channel like HBO or a cable channel, and, if you did not have cable, you could not receive the channel even with an antenna.

2. <u>Guidelines For Off-Air Recording Of Broadcast Programming For Educational Purposes by Non-Profit Educational Institutions</u>

    A.   A broadcast program may be recorded off-air simultaneously with broadcast transmission (including simultaneous cable retransmission) and retained by a non-profit educational institution for a period not to exceed the first forty-five (45) consecutive calendar days after date of recording. Upon conclusion of such retention period, all off-air recordings must be erased or destroyed immediately. "Broadcast programs" are television programs transmitted by television stations for reception by the general public without charge.

ADMINISTRATIVE PROCEDURES

Identification:	Page:	Effective Date:
3.503	2 of 4	September 15, 1992

B.   Off-air recordings may be used once by individual teachers in the course of relevant teaching activities, and repeated once only when instructional reinforcement is necessary, in classrooms and similar places devoted to instruction within a single building, cluster or campus, as well as in the homes of students receiving formalized home instruction, during the first ten (10) consecutive school days in the forty-five (45) calendar day retention period. "School days" are school session days — not counting weekends, holidays, vacations, examination periods, or other scheduled interruptions—within the forty-five (45) calendar day retention period.

C.   Off-air recordings may be made only at the request of and used by individual teachers, and may not be regularly recorded in anticipation of request. No broadcast program may be recorded off-air more than once at the request of the same teacher, regardless of the number of times the program may be broadcast.

D.   A limited number of copies may be reproduced from each off-air recording to meet the legitimate needs of teachers under these guidelines. Each such additional copy shall be subject to all provisions governing the original recording.

E.   After the first ten (10) consecutive school days, off-air recordings may be used up to the end of the forty-five (45) calendar day retention period only for teacher evaluations purposes, i.e. to determine whether or not to include the broadcast program in the teaching curriculum, and may not be used in the recording institution for student exhibition or any other non-evaluation purposes without authorization.

F.   Off-air recordings need not be used in their entirety, but the recorded programs may not be altered from their original content. Off-air recordings may not be physically or electronically combined or merged to constitute teaching anthologies or compilations.

G.   All copies of off-air recordings must include the copyright notice on the broadcast program as recorded.

H.   Educational institutions are expected to establish appropriate control procedures to maintain the integrity of these guidelines. Without such control procedures, no off-air taping is allowed.

ADMINISTRATIVE PROCEDURES

Identification: 3.503	Page: 3 of 4	Effective Date: September 15, 1992

3. Institutional Taping - As per the above "Guidelines," Hillsborough Community College has established the following control procedures:

   A. The guidelines allow off-air taping by an educational institution only, not by an individual. The educational institution representative for these guidelines is the Campus Audiovisual Technician.

   B. The taped programs may not be used for any other purpose except planned, direct, instructional activities, which meet course objectives, in a classroom, and in face-to-face instruction. The taped programs may not be used for entertainment, fund raisers, or time fillers. Any other use, other than instructional, will require a license agreement.

   C. If a faculty member wishes a program that meets educational course objectives to be taped off-air, the faculty member must request this action through the Campus Audiovisual Technician. If television channels are available, the program will be taped and the faculty member notified.

   D. The guidelines go into effect immediately and the tapes will be labeled with deadline information. The faculty member may show the tape in classroom situations for up to ten (10) consecutive school days. On the 11th school day, the tape must be returned to the Campus AV area and can be used for evaluation purposes for another 35 consecutive days. At the end of 45 consecutive days, the tape will be erased.

   E. The faculty member may not make additional copies of the taped program. The LRC may make copies for the convenience of the faculty, but all copies are under the rules of the original and all copies must be returned to be erased at the end of the 45 days.

4. Personal Taping - A program may be taped off-air outside of the Campus AV area under certain circumstances with an HCC-owned tape or personally-owned tape, provided the following criteria are met:

   Remember, off-air does not mean cable; that means no HBO, Discover channel, CNN, etc., unless the channel has offered special permission to teachers. Furthermore, faculty are cautioned not to confuse the following guidelines with the home taping privileges given by the U.S. Supreme Court. In the decision, the Supreme Court declared that the copyright laws do not prohibit off-air recordings by individuals for their personal use in their homes. However, the decision does not permit the use of these tapes outside the home.

ADMINISTRATIVE PROCEDURES

Identification: 3.503	Page: 4 of 4	Effective Date: September 15, 1992

A.   <u>Taping with HCC-owned tape:</u>

    1.   Knowledge of the program requested came to the attention of the faculty member with such short notice that prior arrangements for institutional taping could not be made <u>and/or</u> channels were not available for institutional recording.

    2.   The request to tape must be made by the faculty member to the Campus AV Technician; the faculty request is in the form of a written request for a blank, numbered video tape.

    3.   The faculty member will tape the program off-air and return the program (on the blank tape provided) to the Campus AV Technician (within 24 hours). The guidelines go into effect at that time.

    4.   Upon receipt of the tape, the Campus AV Technician will log in the tape and place a label on the tape indicating date of recording and date of erasure. The faculty member will be reminded at that time of the classroom viewing restrictions noted in the guidelines.

B.   <u>Taping with personally-owned tape</u> - A faculty member is not allowed to use in the classroom a video program taped off-air that does not follow the above procedures. Extenuating circumstances may be discussed with the Copyright Officer who may authorize an exception by allowing the faculty member to use his/her own tape with the understanding that the tape will become the temporary property of Hillsborough Community College within 24 hours after taping, at which time the guidelines go into effect. Once the tape has been erased, it will be returned to the faculty member.

SAMPLE

REQUEST FOR OFF-AIR BROADCAST PROGRAM RECORDING

I, the undersigned:

1. Request the N.C.C.C. Communication Technology Center to record the following television program(s) as listed below in accordance to the Guidelines for Off-Air Recording of Broadcast Programming as outlined in the N.C.C.C. Copyright Policy.

2. Acknowledge said policy. (see reverse)

3. Agree to accept responsibility for the use and return of this video material to the CTC for erasure to prevent any infringement of copyright law unless express written consent from the copyright holder is obtained for conditional program retention.

Title of Program to be Recorded_____

_____

Date of Recording_____

Length of Program_____

Date Program is Needed: Special Instructions_____

_____

Requestor's Name_____

Department & Extension #_____

Erasure Date_____

SAMPLE

Appended to College copyright informational guide

North Country Community College

Permitted Uses   NCCC Instructors/personnel **MAY:**

a. record or request the recording of an off-air broadcast program (must be recorded in its entirety with copyright notice and includes simultaneous cable/satellite transmissions) for short-term immediate use (one regular showing and one reinforcement showing within 10 consecutive school days from the original recording date. PBS programs must be used within 7 consecutive school days from original recording date)

b. retain the program for an additional 35 days for evaluative purposes for purchase consideration for a total of 45 days (PBS 42 days) from the original recording date. After the 45/42 day period expires, the recording <u>must</u> be returned to and erased by CTC personnel

c. record or request an off-air broadcast program for his or her use only

d. request limited copies of the same program to meet their legitimate instructional needs. These copies are also to be retained only within the 45/42 day total period

e. contact the copyright holder for permission to secure recording/retention rights either through written permission or outright purchase. (See "Television and Cable Networks List" to contact program producers.)

Prohibited Uses   NCCC Instructors/personnel **MAY NOT:**

a. request or record off-air broadcast programs in anticipation of future (as opposed to immediate) needs or requests

b. record or request tapings of off-air broadcast programs more than once for any instructor regardless of the number of times the program is broadcasted

c. use or retain a recorded off-air broadcast program after the 45/42 day retention period has expired for any reasons including technical difficulties or class showing scheduling problems

d. request or record off-air broadcast programs that are specifically prohibited from being recorded by notice of the copyright holder

e. request or record only portions of an off-air broadcast program. The program must be recorded in its entirety *including* its copyright notice

f. alter the original content of the recorded program by physical or electronic manipulation to form teaching anthologies or derivative works.

SAMPLE

North Country Community College

SAMPLE

PRODUCER INQUIRY LETTER FOR
OFF-AIR BROADCAST RECORDING
[*Use official NCCC letterhead for inquiry*]

Date

Network Corporate Home Address (ABC, CBS, FOX, NBC, PBS)

Permission Department

I am requesting information on the availability and retention of the following

program:

Title..Air Date.....................

Can a copy of this program be retained for classroom instructional use?

(Circle)   **Yes**   **No**

Is this program available for sale?

(Circle)   **Yes**   **No**

　　　　If yes, please specify agency distributing this program:

....

Please specify format...Cost (if known).....................

Enclosed is a self-addressed, stamped envelope for your convenience in replying to

this request. Should you be unable to authorize this request, or provide the above

information, please forward this letter to the appropriate person or agency.

Sincerely,

＊＊

Permission to retain off-air copy on a free basis:

Authorized by...Title...............................

Date...........................

Conditions (if any)..

SAMPLE

The following agency deals with "pre-approved" copying of certain titles for academic institutions and commercial organizations. It is a central rights/royalty clearinghouse.

Copyright Clearance Center
Academic Permission Service
27 Congress Street
Salem, MA 01970

Address for performance rights organizations:

American Society of Composers, Authors, & Publishers (ASCAP)
One Lincoln Plaza
New York, NY 10019

Broadcast Music, Inc. (BMI)
40 West 57th Street
New York, NY 10019

Society of European Stage Authors and Composers, Inc. (SESAC)
156 W. 56th Street
New York, NY 10019

Dramatico-musical works: write to publisher or one of the following agencies:

Tams-Witmark Music Library, Inc.
757 Third Avenue
New York, NY 10017

Music Theatre International
119 West 57th Street
New York, NY 10019

Rogers & Hammerstein Library
598 Madison Avenue
New York, NY 10022

Samuel French, Inc.
25 West 45th Street
New York, NY 10036

The following agency handles recording rights for most music publishers:

The Harry Fox Agency
205 East 42nd Street
New York, NY 10017

TELEVISION & CABLE NETWORKS LIST

The following is a list of television and cable networks that may be used to secure licenses of programs that you may wish to record off-air or which you have already recorded off-air under the Off-Air Recording of Broadcast Programming Guidelines.

The guidelines allow NCCC instructors/personnel to record off-air from regular broadcast networks and do not include programs from cable channels. It is highly recommended that you contact each cable network in order to determine the nature of their policies regarding off-air taping for educational purposes.

Under no circumstances should you request this information from individual stations or cable operators as they do not have the right to grant permission unless they own the program (which is not a common occurrence). The stations may be able to put you in touch with the copyright holder.

NETWORK TELEVISION:

ABC	(212) 456-7777	77 W 66th St., 9th Floor, New York, NY 10023
CBS	(212) 975-4321	51 W 52nd St., New York, NY 10019
FOX	(213) 277-2211	P.O. Box 900, Beverly Hills, CA 90213
NBC	(212) 664-4444	30 Rockefeller Plaza, 25th Floor, New York, NY 10112
PBS	(703) 739-5038	1320 Braddock Place, Alexandria, VA 22314

CABLE TELEVISION:

A & E   Arts and Entertainment Network
          (212) 210-9725   P.O. Box 1610, Grand Central Station, NY, NY 10163-1610
AMC   American Movie Classics
          (516) 364-2222   150 Crossways Park West, Woodbury, NY 11797
BET   Black Entertainment Television
          (800) 229-2388   1700 Moore Street, Ste 2200, Rosslyn, VA 22201
BRV   Bravo
          (516) 364-2222   150 Crossways Park West, Woodbury, NY 11797
CNBC   Consumer News and Business Channel
          (201) 585-2622   2200 Fletcher Avenue, Ft. Lee, NJ 07024
CNN   Cable News Network
          (800) 344-6219   1 CNN Center, Box 105366, Atlanta, GA 30348
COM   Comedy Central
          (212) 408-8500   1775 Broadway, New York, NY 10019
C-SPAN   Cable-Satellite Public Affairs Network
          (800) 523-7586   400 N Capitol Street, Ste. 650, Washington, DC 20001
CTN   Courtroom Television Network
          (212) 973-2800   Merrill Brown, 600 Third Avenue, New York, NY 10016
DIS   Disney Channel
          (818) 569-7500   3800 W Alameda Ave, Burbank, CA 91505
ENC   Encore
          (213) 393-3745   100 Wilshire Blvd, Suite 1600, Santa Monica, CA 90401
ESPN   Entertainment and Sports Network
          (203) 585-2236   ESPN Plaza, 935 Middle Street, Bristol, CT 06010

FAM   The Family Channel
         (804) 323-7301   1000 Centerville Turnpike, Virginia Beach, VA 23463
GALA   Galavision

                          2121 Ave of the Stars, Suite 2300, Los Angeles, CA 90067
HBO   Home Box Office
         (212) 512-1000   1100 Ave of the Americas, New York, NY 10036
LIFE   Lifetime
         (718) 452-4000   3612 35th Ave, Astoria, NY 11106
MAX   Cinemax
         (212) 512-1000   1100 Ave of the Americas, New York, NY 10036
ME/U   Mind Extension University
         (800) 777-6463   9697 E Mineral Ave, Englewood, CO 80112
MTV   Music Television
         (212) 713-6400   1775 Broadway, New York, NY 10019
NICK   Nickelodeon
         (212) 258-7500   1515 Broadway, New York, NY 10036
SC   Sports Channel
         (716) 524-9444   820 W Madison, Oak Park, IL 60302
SHOW   Showtime
         (312) 983-0100   444 N Lakeshore, Chicago, IL 60611
TBS   Turner Broadcasting System (Super Station)
         (800) 344-6219   Turner Educational Services, 1 CNN Ctr., Atlanta, GA 30348
TDC   The Discovery Channel
         (301) 986-0444   7700 Wisconsin Ave, Bethesda, MD 20814-3522
TLC   The Learning Channel
         (800) 321-1832   7700 Wisconsin Ave, Bethesda, MD 20814-3522
TMC   The Movie Channel
         (212) 708-1600   1633 Broadway, New York, NY 10019
TNN   The Nashville Network
         (615) 883-7000   2805 Opryland Drive, Nashville, TN 37214
TNT   Turner Network Television
         (800) 344-6219   1CNN Center, Box 105366, Atlanta, GA 30348-5366
TRAV   The Travel Channel
         (212) 603-4549   1370 Ave of the Americas, New York, NY 10019
TWC   The Weather Channel
         (404) 434-6800   2600 Cumberland Pkwy, Atlanta, GA 30339
UNI   Univision
         (212) 455-5309   605 3rd Ave, New York, NY 10158
USA   USA Network
         (212) 408-9100   1230 Ave of the Americas, New York, NY 10020
VH-1   Video Hits 1
         (212) 713-6458   1775 Broadway, New York, NY 10019
VISN   Vision Interfaith Satellite Network
         (800) 841-VISN   74 Trinity Place, 8th Floor, New York, NY 10006
WOR   Chicago Super Station
         (201) 330-2154   9 Broadcast Plaza, Secaucus, NY 07096

Listing provided courtesy of Association for Media & Equipment (AIME), Elkader, IA.

SPRINGFIELD TECHNICAL COMMUNITY COLLEGE   LIBRARY
SPRINGFIELD, MASSACHUSETTS 01101   AUDIOVISUAL DEPT

OFF-AIR TAPING REQUEST

FACULTY_____   DEPT_____

COURSE TITLE_____   COURSE NO._____

DATE OF REQUEST_____

TITLE OF PROGRAM_____

AIR DATE_____   NETWORK/STATION_____   TIME_____

DATE TO BE USED_____

Off-air taping is done in accordance with the guidelines developed by the Negotiating Committee of the US House Subcommittee on Courts, Civil Liberties and Administration of Justice. The guidelines were developed in line with the "FAIR USE" provision of the 1976 Copyright Law.

The following is a brief synopsis of the guidelines:

1. Off-air taping permitted to non-profit educational institutions only.
2. Off-air tape can be retained for 45 calendar days from air date then <u>must be</u> <u>erased or</u> <u>destroyed</u>.
3. Off-air tape can be <u>shown once within 10 consecutive school days</u> from air date by and instructor in a location normally used for eductional purposes.
4. It may be repeated once within the 10 consecutive school days from air date for purposes of reinforcement.
5. The 45 calendar day retention period is for the purpose of evaluation only.
6. An individual instructor may only make one request for a particular program.

For more detailed information please speak with the AV Librarian.

Springfield Technical Community College

William Rainey Harper College

1200 West Algonquin Road
Palatine, Illinois 60067-7398
708-397-3000

TO:

RE: Copyright Provision for Copyright Law effective January 1, 1978. Would you provide us with your company's policies regarding use and duplication of your materials indicated on our P.O. # _____.
Title(s) listed on order are:

1. May we make two copies for the purposes of closed and/or open captioning? _____
2. May we make an archival copy? _____
3. Under what conditions may we duplicate copies of the materials for educational use only?_____
4. If duplication is not permitted, do you provide a discount price for additional copies?
   _____
5. May we use the materials on an educational TV channel:
   Closed circuit within the school? _____
   Educational channel on community cable system? _____
6. How long is this policy in effect?
   For one year _____   Indefinitely _____ .   Other_____

Copyright changes have affected us all, and we want to be responsible. Please assist us by returning this form promptly. If you do not hold copyright, please forward a copy of this purchase order with this form to the copyright holder.

Thank you,

Mary L. Severs

Mary Severs
Coordinator of Technical Services
Harper College Library

MediaPermissionRequest
PimaCountyCommunityCollegeDistrict

Date:

To:

Dear Media Producer:

Regarding the material titled, _____ .
We would like to have permission to do one or more of the following:

☐ Retain a copy of the material which we have recorded off-air beyond the seven-day limit. We would like to

retain the material until _____ for classroom use only.

☐ Make a permanent copy of a tape we own, for classroom use only.

☐ Make a temporary copy of tape we own, for classroom use only. The material would be retained until

_____ .

☐ Make a "backup" copy of a tape we own. The copy would only be sued in case of irreparable damage to our
original tape, and only until a replacement copy could be purchased.

☐ Make a format change. We own the material in the format listed below, but would like permission to make a

copy in another format. We would like to change from: _____

to: _____ .

☐ Play the material over Pima Community College channels on Tucson area cable systems. The material

would be cablecast for the purpose of _____

beginning _____ and ending _____ , and shown a

total of _____ times.

☐ Use a portion of this material in a videotape we are producing (as described below).

☐ Other:

Sincerely,

Name: _____

Title: _____

Phone: (520) _____ Fax: (520) 748-4990

Please send your response to this request to: *Office of Policy & Library Technology*
Pima Community College
4905C East Broadway Boulevard
Tucson, Arizona 85709-1130

Pima County Community College

Broome Community College
P.O. Box 1017
Binghamton, NY 13902

COPYRIGHT PERMISSION REQUEST FOR DUPLICATION OR ADAPTATION

To: _____ From: _____

_____ Date: _____

_____

We hereby request permission to duplicate, adapt, or use copyrighted materials for the project described below. This project will be used exclusively for educational purposes, with no direct or indirect commercial advantage, and will include credit for your work.

Title of Copyrighted Material: _____

Author: _____

Publisher: _____ Copyright Date: _____

Material to be duplicated or adapted: _____

Type of reproduction or adaptation: _____

Number of copies: _____

Use to be made of material: _____

_____

_____

Distribution of copies: _____

Please indicate your permission below and return this form within two weeks from the above date. A return envelope is enclosed for your convenience.

☐ Permission granted.

☐ Permission granted with the following restrictions:_____

_____

☐ Permission denied. (If so, is there another means by which we can obtain this material for our project?)

☐ Alternate Source: _____

Name *(Printed)* _____ Title _____

Signature   Broome Community College _____ Date _____

LRC Media Services

Copyright Acknowledgement

I, _____ , realize that use of copyrighted music or

materials in my _____

(Name of Class)

class project tentatively titled _____

limits the showing of this project to my class presentation only. All other showings are in violation of the United States
Copyright Law.

Signed: _____

Date:_____

Education Network of Maine
Copyright/Broadcast Policies and Procedures

It is the expectation that employees of the Education Network of Maine and faculty using distance education technologies will adhere to the provision of the current copyright law (Title 17, United State Code). The basic intent of the copyright law is to ensure that ownership rights to copyrighted materials are protected. The accompanying policy is not intended to stand alone, but to serve as a guide and as a means of preventing copyright violations.

I. Infringement of Copyright -- How to Avoid It

Generally speaking, it is an infringement of the copyright laws for any person other than the copyright owner to:

1. Give permission to broadcast
2. Make copies (or have copies made)
3. Prepare derivative works (such as an anthology or a coursepack)
4. Perform the works publicly

To perform any of these functions, permission must be given by the copyright holder.

II.   Responsibility for Complying With Laws

Each University campus or transmission site will designate an individual to assist faculty and staff in determining when permission from copyright owners is needed for ITV broadcasts. The Copyright Designee will contact the appropriate authority in an effort to obtain permission for any instructional purpose on the ITV system. The final responsibility for obtaining copyright permission to broadcast any materials lies with the individual instructor or staff member wishing to use the instructional material over the ITV system.

III.   General Steps to be Followed for Obtaining Broadcast Rights

- Faculty or staff member consults with the copyright designee at his/her university campus or transmission site for the purpose of obtaining recommendations for learning materials to supplement course content.

- ITV or instructional design staff are contacted for assistance in selecting formats and items for broadcast. All materials must be displayed in the original format for which the copyright permission was obtained.

University of Maine at Augusta

- Once material to be used in the course is identified, a faculty or staff member will request the copyright designee (for the Education Network, it is Susan Lowe) to evaluate the copyright conditions and recommend a course of action.

- The copyright designee will attempt to obtain broadcast rights clearance, arrange the necessary paperwork, billing and payment, to achieve a copyright release.

- Copyright permission must be obtained prior to using any material over the ITV system. If the copyright holder cannot be contacted or refuses to grant release, that material cannot be used on the ITV system.

- Copyright authorization forms will be maintained in the copyright designee's files at the university campus or broadcast site. **No audio/visual support materials will be broadcast without either an attached authorization letter or appearing on the cleared audiovisual materials list. Cable courses require additional clearance and should be checked on a case-by-case basis.**

- If an ITV technician receives audiovisual material to be broadcast which does not either have an authorization letter or appear on the cleared list, they will notify the instructor or staff member of the copyright clearance procedures.

V. Other General Clarifications

- Off-air recordings cannot be used over the ITV system unless the item has been purchased or permission to air has been granted using the standard copyright release form and procedures.

- For materials owned by the instructor or staff member, the copyright designee will determine if the material is a legal copy.

- Rented material such as rented videotapes cannot be used without copyright permission. Basically, you must own the material and obtain permission.
- Maps, if used in their original form, are acceptable without copyright permission. However, if the material is manipulated, then the general guidelines for obtaining copyright permission must be followed.

- Music can be used only if it (1) relates to the curriculum and (2) it is played in its original (purchased) form. Copying or creating anthologies can only be done by first obtaining copyright permission.

- Computer databases, WEB sites, and software requires copyright permission and, therefore, the basic guidelines apply.

- Text and related support material if used in its original format (for that matter, any printed material) does not require special copyright permission for broadcast over the ITV system. However, any manipulation or duplication of any printed material requires special copyright clearance and should be discussed with the copyright designee. The use of any audiovisual support materials (such as a videodisc) that may accompany a textbook must also be reviewed for copyright clearance.

VI. Other Considerations

- The standard release used states that ITV class tapes will be erased at the end of each semester. Additional copyright permission must be obtained for any tapes kept beyond the original semester. Duplication of the tapes must also follow copyright clearance procedures. If an instructor or staff member wishes to keep a videotape copy of any course lecture, all copyright permissions must be renegotiated through the copyright designee.

c:\copright\policy
rev. 06/13/96
sl

UNIVERSITY OF MAINE *at Augusta*

Education Network of Maine

University Heights
Augusta, Maine 04330-9410
(207) 621-3301
FAX: 1-800-696-1125 In State
207-621-3420 Out of State

Date: _____

To:

REQUEST FOR AUTHORIZATION TO USE AUDIOVISUAL MATERIAL OVER UNIVERSITY OF MAINE'S INTERACTIVE TELEVISION SYSTEM

To comply with federal copyright laws, we must have on file, written authorization for the use of _____

_____

for use in our Interactive <u>Instructional</u> Television System which connects the University of Maine campuses and several off-campus sites. Courses originate at one of the campuses and are received at other locations in specially adapted television classrooms. Classes are conducted at specified times and days and are recorded on VHS tape for students' review. The tapes are held for limited periods in the library at the classroom locations, then erased. Students must be on site in order to participate in classes or to review. TAPES DO NOT CIRCULATE OUTSIDE THE LIBRARIES. THIS MATERIAL IS USED FOR EDUCATIONAL PURPOSES ONLY.

AUTHORIZATION FOR THE ABOVE USE:

Approved by: _____

Title:_____

Any Conditions/Fees _____

If you have questions or need additional information, please call Kirk T. Rau, Assistant Director of Learning Resource Center, (207) 621-3341.

The Community College of the University of Maine System

University of Maine at Augusta

UNIVERSITY OF MAINE *at Augusta*

Education Network of Maine

University Heights
Augusta, Maine 04330-9410
(207) 621-3301
FAX: 1-800-696-1125 In State
207-621-3420 Out of State

Date: _____

To:

REQUEST FOR AUTHORIZATION TO USE AUDIOVISUAL MATERIAL OVER UNIVERSITY OF MAINE'S INTERACTIVE TELEVISION SYSTEM

To comply with federal copyright laws, we must have on file, written authorization for the use of _____

_____

for use in our Interactive <u>Instructional</u> Television System which connects the University of Maine campuses and several off-campus sites. Courses originate at one of the campuses and are received at other locations in specially adapted television classrooms. Classes are conducted at specified times and days and are recorded on VHS tape for students' review. The tapes are held for limited periods in the library at the classroom locations, then erased. Students must be on site in order to participate in classes or to review. TAPES CIRCULATE OUTSIDE THE LIBRARIES FOR A LIMITED PERIOD OF TIME. THIS MATERIAL IS USED FOR EDUCATIONAL PURPOSES ONLY.

AUTHORIZATION FOR THE ABOVE USE:

Approved by: _____

Title:_____

Any Conditions/Fees _____

If you have questions or need additional information, please call Kirk T. Rau, Assistant Director of Learning Resource Center, (207) 621-3341.

The Community College of the University of Maine System

University of Maine at Augusta

Printed on Recycled Paper

TABLE OF CONTENTS

A PRIMER ON DISTANCE LEARNING AND INTELLECTUAL PROPERTY ISSUES

DOW, LOHNES & ALBERTSON
1200 New Hampshire Ave. NW
Suite 800
Washington, D.C. 20036
Telephone (202) 776-2000
Facsimile (202) 776-2222

Appendix B

DL&A
Dow, Lohnes & Albertson

A Primer on Distance Learning
and Intellectual Property Issues

Kenneth D. Salomon, Esquire
Dow, Lohnes & Albertson
Washington, D.C.

MARCH, 1994

Northwest Michigan College

I. INTRODUCTION

A. The Distance Learning Environment

Dramatic advances in communications technology have created many exciting and informational programming opportunities. Academic institutions, either individually or as part of networks, now use satellite and other technologies to distribute instructional programming ("telecourses") and share research findings on a regional, national, and even international basis. Persons working in remote locations or at full-time jobs or studying at widely dispersed campuses benefit from "distance learning" by taking courses and earning college degrees, continuing education credits or job site training via telecommunications.

Several of the organizations distributing instructional programming via telecommunications also produce programs on a small scale. Students unable to view the instructional programs at the regularly scheduled times may view videotapes recorded at network headquarters or at receive sites. Programmers often insert separate audio and video materials, such as excerpts of articles, diagrams, charts and graphs, into the programs for greater educational impact.

Educational organizations have begun to utilize the very latest in communications technologies, such as Integrated Services Digital Networks (ISDN), which promise to increase the real-time interactive capability of educational networks. Many students who participate in "distance learning" interact with instructors through two-way audio, telephone, facsimile, computer mail and traditional mail.

II. COPYRIGHT BASICS

A. Copyright and Ownership Rights

Under the Copyright Act of 1976 ("Copyright Act" or "Act"), copyright attaches automatically to a work at the time it is "fixed in a tangible medium." Therefore, any outlines or scripts used in connection with classroom instruction enjoy some copyright protection as soon as they are written. Similarly, the lectures themselves receive copyright protection once they are taped or otherwise recorded in a permanent medium.

For works created by an individual, copyright lasts for the life of the author plus fifty years. For works created by an individual for someone else, i.e. "for hire," copyright lasts for a period of one hundred years from the creation of the work or seventy-five years from its publication whichever is earlier. Publication involves loaning, leasing, selling or giving away copies of a work. It should be noted that, while satellite distribution of a work represents "public performance" under the Copyright Act, it does not constitute publication. If, however, copies of the program are made and later distributed, this qualifies as publication.

During the period of copyright protection, copyright owners have the exclusive right to (1) reproduce the copyrighted work; (2) prepare derivative works based on the copyrights work; (3) publish the work by distributing copies to the public by sale, rental, lease or lending; (4) publicly perform the copyrighted work; and (5) publicly display the work. Copyright owners may transfer these exclusive rights to others, either as individual rights or as an entire "bundle of rights."[1]

1 A transfer of copyright ownership is defined under the Copyright Act as "an assignment, mortgage, exclusive license, or any other conveyance, alienation, or hypothecation of a copyright or of any of the exclusive rights comprised in a copyright, whether or not it is limited in time or place of effect, but not including a nonexclusive license." 17 U.S.C. 101. Transfers, which must be in writing and signed by the party making the transfer, should be recorded with the Copyright Office. Recording the transfer provides constructive notice of the transfer and is also a prerequisite to an infringement suit.

B. Copyright Issues and Distance Learning

Virtually every operational aspect of a telecommunications-based educational network creates its own important intellectual property issues. Many organizations, however, do not consider copyright issues until forced to do so by litigious copyright owners; controversies frequently arise upon discovery of a lucrative aftermarket for copyrighted works. Entities involved in the telecommunications distribution of educational or instructional programming will profit, therefore, by anticipating and planning for such issues rather than dealing with them as an afterthought.

This primer highlights the intellectual property issues that will inevitably confront telecommunication networks, participating universities, and other programming contributors who produce and distribute educational programming via telecommunications. The primer also suggests measures that can help shield these entities from copyright liability while permitting maximum flexibility for the exploitation of educational programming.

C. The National Information Infrastructure

This primer should also be read in the context of the effort by the Clinton Administration to facilitate creation of the "electronic superhighway." Under the guidance of the Department of Commerce, the National Information Infrastructure Task Force will be addressing not only the issues of technology, but also the uses of information. Vital policy questions concerning ownership and exploitation of information, as well as privacy and piracy, will be addressed. This initiative is already underway. In the coming months, distance learning professionals should position themselves to become key participants in this debate.

Northwest Michigan College

B. Copyright Registration, Notice and Damages

Over the course of recent years, the legal importance of registration has been reduced. While registration of a work with the Copyright Office is no longer mandatory and may be made at any time during the term of copyright, registration still establishes a clear public record of the copyright claim. Also, if registration is made before or within five years of publication, it constitutes prima facie evidence of copyright validity.

In order to register a work, copyright owners must complete an application form, pay a filing fee (currently $20.00), and deposit copies of their works with the Copyright Office. Since the instructional programming produced by most telecommunications organizations is not widely available to the general public, the appropriate entity may organize its copyrightable material in any manner it deems convenient (e.g. by semester, by year, by course or group of courses, by university, etc.).

Although copyright attaches upon creation, copyright owners should register and affix the appropriate notice (in the form of "(insert copyright symbol) 1991 John Doe") to all works in order to advise the public of their copyright. While copyright notice is optional for works first published on or after March 1, 1989, it is highly recommended.[2]

Notice informs the public that the work is protected by copyright, identifies the copyright owner, and shows the year of first publication. Furthermore, the defendant in an infringement

action cannot claim that he or she was an "innocent infringer" of a work if the work bears the proper notice. A court will usually reduce damages in cases where a defendant successfully claims innocent infringement. Copyright owners do not need to register the work with the Copyright Office or obtain its permission prior to affixing the copyright notice. The notice should appear at the beginning and end of all telecourse program transmissions, and on all copies distributed to the public through any secondary medium, such as video cassettes. In addition, telecommunications organizations and/or participating universities should contractually require any transferee to guarantee that it will include proper notice on all programming distributed in any form.

Copyright owners may recover statutory damages in lieu of actual damages and profits, as well as attorney's fees. Statutory damages may range from $500 to $20,000 per work infringed (up to $100,000 in cases of willful infringement). However, if the defendant establishes its infringement was "innocent," then statutory damages may be reduced to $200 per work. For non-profit educational institutions, libraries, archives or their employees, statutory damages may be remitted if the infringer had an honest belief and reasonable grounds that the use of the copyrighted works was a "fair use."

---

2 Any work first published before March 1, 1989 risks losing protection unless it bears a notice of copyright. However, copyright is not automatically lost if notice was omitted or an error was made on copies distributed between January 1, 1978 and March 1, 1989. Copyright protection extends to works registered within five years after publication without notice, if the owner makes a reasonable effort after discovery of the omission to add notice to all copies distributed in the United States.

reproduce any derivative works prepared from those materials. Groups should also obtain clearances for all ancillary materials distributed to students in connection with the telecast courses. Although sections of the Copyright Act allow for the use of certain materials without the copyright owner's permission in face-to-face teaching situations and in transmitted classes, the scope of this permission is somewhat unclear. These provisions are discussed in greater detail below. Therefore, it is recommended that careful assessment be made of the availability for the intended use of copyrighted works and when doubts about entitlement to use persist, permission be obtained. Absent such agreements, telecommunications organizations and their universities may be liable for copyright infringement.[3]

Moreover, an otherwise permissible use of materials in the face-to-face classroom setting may expose telecommunications organizations and universities to liability when telecourses are transmitted and/or recorded at remote receive sites for later use. Finally, while universities may already have agreements that expressly authorize the use of certain materials for classroom purposes, it may well be that these agreements are not broad enough to accommodate telecommunications transmission, videotape recording, or the distributiom of course-related materials beyond the classroom setting.

3 The copyright Act specifically provides that states may not rely upon the U S Constitution's 11th Amendment immunity clause to escape copyright liability for their infringements

III. COPYRIGHT OWNERSHIP PROBLEMS PARTICULAR TO TELECOMMUNICATIONS DISTRIBUTED EDUCATIONAL MATERIAL

A. Introduction

Copyright law provides a general framework for determining the ownership of various intellectual property rights. Although the law regarding general interest programming is relatively well settled, complex questions concerning copyright ownership arise when telecourses integrate live lectures and pre-existing materials. The ownership picture is further clouded when groups record programs for tape delayed viewing and archiving.

As a general rule, parties should enter into written agreements with producers, professors, students and all other contributors. Each agreement should specifically delineate the ownership of intellectual property rights in the programming itself and the materials integrated into the programming. Absent such agreements, ownership questions could ultimately be decided through litigation.

B. Agreements with Contributors

1. Use of Underlying Materials

a. Transmission and Distribution of Works Created or Owned by Others

Before producing or distributing any programming that incorporates the copyrighted works of others, telecommunications organizations and universities should obtain written clearances from copyright owners that allow the entities to perform, display, distribute and reproduce all visual, musical and written material incorporated within the programming and to prepare, perform, display, distribute and

same programs and related materials in subsequent semesters or years. In addition, the defense applies only to materials that are copied at the behest of professors or by professors themselves. Furthermore, book publishers have successfully sued university copy centers for photocopying even at a professor's request. The fair use defense, may not, therefore, protect all copying done by telecommunications organizations, independent producers, corporations, or universities. Finally, fair use may not permit any subsequent "for-profit" marketing of the programming that embodies the copied material.

c. Non-Profit Educational Exemptions to Copyright Infringement

Section 110(1) of the Copyright Act permits the performance or display of a copyrighted work "in the course of face-to-face teaching activities . . . in a classroom or similar place devoted to instruction". Due to its in-class restrictions, however, this provision may not protect the telecommunications transmission and likely does not protect the subsequent videotaping of programming embodying copyrighted works. While Section 110(2) does specifically exempt the performance and display of certain materials that are transmitted for instructional purposes, this exemption does not apply to any copying or later distribution of programs.

In summary, neither the Act's fair use defense nor its non-profit educational exemptions will completely insulate telecommunications organizations and universities that produce, distribute and videotape programming from copyright infringement charges. Organizations and universities should, therefore, obtain written clearances permitting the use of materials inserted into educational programming and for materials distributed in connection with the programming. These agreements should cover initial transmission, any subsequent copying and the lending of videotaped copies to students for later viewing and, if possible, future uses as well.

b. The Fair Use Defense

The Copyright Act permits a "fair use" defense to a charge of copyright infringement when the unauthorized use is made for purposes of teaching, scholarship, research, criticism or comment. Significantly, "fair use" is not a bright line legal test. Rather, four statutory criteria are assessed. They are:

1) The purpose and character of the use (including whether it is for profit or not)
2) The nature of the copyrighted work
3) The substantiality of the amount used in comparison to the total work
4) The effect of the use on the marketability of the original

Due to the potential ambiguities inherent in a fair use analysis, telecommunications organizations and their member universities should hesitate before relying upon the fair use defense.[4] To help educators, certain non-statutory guidelines covering educational photocopying were agreed to at the time the Act was passed in 1976. In 1981, the guidelines were expanded to cover video material. Nevertheless, application of the fair use criteria requires a complex legal analysis which, at best, often provides contradictory answers. In addition, the defense may not protect many of the contemplated distribution scenarios. For example, the 1976 guidelines stated that a fair use would not protect the use of material by the same instructor "from term to term"; this prohibition would, arguably, preclude organizations and universities from distributing the

Northwest Michigan College

4 The fair use defense will only apply to the materials used for instructional purposes. Thus, for example, 'bridge music' may not be exempted where its only purpose is to enhance the ambiance of a program or to fill time in between programs

1. Collective Work Model

A copyrightable work may arise from the collection of other, individually copyrighted works. Under this "collective work" model, a telecommunications organization would own an entire program (as a "collective work"), while individual contributors would own their specific presentations. Unless contributors expressly transferred their rights to the organizations or participating universities, however, these entities could only reproduce and distribute the program in its entirety and would be restricted in exploiting the various contributions.

2. Joint Work Model

The Act also recoginzes ownership for a "joint work" in which multiple authors merge their contributions into a single, inseparable work. A telecourse could thus be considered jointly created and telecommunications organizations, universities and individual contributors would hold joint ownership. Joint owners may individually exploit the work, subject to a proper accounting to the other copyright owners for profits earned from the work. This status could complicate the granting of exclusive rights in the works to third parties.

3. Works Made for Hire Model

The Copyright Act also recognizes that materials may be created as "works for hire," for the telecommunications organization or university and, therefore, would be solely owned by those organizations. Works created "for hire" are those prepared by an employee within the scope of his or her employment; alternatively, any work that is specially ordered or commissioned as part of a collective work, audiovisual work or as an instructional text is a work for hire if the party signs a written instrument to that effect. It is, therefore, important that

2. Scripts and Lecture Notes

The act specifically grants the copyright owner the exclusive right to make derivative works from an original copyrighted work. Therefore, contributors to instructional programming may claim ownership rights to the programming itself under the theory that the program is a "derivative work of their lecture notes or other materials." Accordingly, telecommunications organizations and educational institutions should consider requiring instructors and other contributors to relinquish copyright ownership rights to any notes or other materials from which their presentations are delivered.

3. Student Waivers

Other classroom participants, aside from lecturers and contributors, may also be able to make a claim regarding telecourses. In order to be protected fully, telecommunication organizations and universities should obtain a release from all students, or other audience members, as well as lecturers and other "on-camera" participants, that assign their contributions in the work to the organization or university and authorize the use of their name, voice and likeness. This release protects the organizations and the universities from claims by classroom participants or lecturers for invasion of privacy, interference with the right of publicity and copyright infringement.

C. Copyright Ownership Models

Absent express agreements, the Copyright Act itself may order intellectural property ownership arrangements between telecommunications educational networks, member corporations and participating universities, independent producers and individual contributors.

expressly state that organizations and/or universities are autorized to copy and distribute programming for "any and all purposes" and "by means of any and all existing technologies and any and all technologies hereinafter created."

B. International Distribution

Telecommunications organizations and participating universities contemplating satellite distribution, videocassette sales, or interactive teleconferencing on an international scale must be aware of the significant differences between United States copyright law and the copyright laws of other countries. Telecommunications organizations and universities considering any type of foreign venture should familiarize themselves with (1) the basic terms of the two major international copyright treaties and (2) the copyright law of the nations in which their programming will be distributed.

While there is no such thing as an "international copyright" that will universally protect intellectual property rights, most countries afford U.S. copyright owners some protection under the terms of the two major international copyright conventions to which the United States belongs: the Universal Copyright Convention ("UCC") and the Berne Convention for the Protection of Literacy and Artistic Works ("Berne").

Generally, an author may claim protection for a work under the UCC if he is a national or domiciliary of a country that is a member of the UCC or if the work was first published in a UCC country. The work must, however, bear the notice of copyright in the form and position specified by the UCC. The UCC notice consists of the symbol "C," the name of the copyright owner and the year the work was first published.

telecommunications organizations and universities enter into an agreement with a contributor that specifically states that the materials are created as works made for hire or, alternatively, that assigns the copyrights to the organization or university.

D. Summary

At a minimum, any agreement between a telecommunications organization or university and its program contributors must state that the organization has the right to transmit the programs by means of telecommunications for performance within a classroom or classroom-type setting, that particular universities or businesses have the right to copy and distribute the programs for a limited time, and that the parties will negotiate in good faith regarding any further distribution rights. For greater protection, contributors should be asked to sign an agreement explicitly stating that the works were created for hire or that any and all copyrights are transferred to the telecommunications organization or university. As a reminder, all such transfers should be recorded with the Copyright Office at the Library of Congress.

IV. EXPANDING SERVICES INTO FUTURE MARKETS: COPYRIGHT PROBLEMS

A. Future Technologies

Intellectual property ownership problem will most likely materialize when audience size or revenue potential increases, or when the traditional medium of distribution changes. A well-drafted agreement should recognize and provide for these contingencies. In order to ensure that distribution rights will not be limited to the initial transmission, agreements should

Berne-member countries treat U.S. copyright owners like their own nationals for copyright purposes. A work first published in the United States or another Berne country (or first published in a non-Berne country, followed by publication within thirty days in a Berne country) is automatically eligible for protection in all Berne member countries.

V. TRADEMARK ISSUES

In addition to insuring against copyright infringement claims, organizations and universities should protect their trademark rights by registering any trademarks or service marks which are currently in use or which may be used in the near future for "distance learning" goods or services. The system of federal registration, which categorizes marks into forty-two classes of goods and services, protects trademark rights nationwide.

Federal registration lasts for ten years and may be renewed. Registrants are required to complete an application, submit samples ("specimens") of their mark to the Trademark Office, indicate the date on which they first used the mark and pay a filing fee of $245 per mark per class.[5] After five years, trademark owners must affirm their continued use of a mark; the trademark then achieves "incontestable" status, offering even greater protection for the trademark holder.[6]

Organizations and universities may also choose to supplement a federal registration with individual state registrations. Although the state registration procedure is faster than federal registration (it can take up to twelve months to process federal filings, while state filing may be handled in two to four weeks) the value of a state registration is limited. Nevertheless, state registrations provide additional public notice which may be beneficial in cases of disputes. International registrations are also vital to U.S. businesses which operate overseas. Since many foreign nations employ a "first to file" system of protection, prompt action may be necessary to ensure unimpeded use of trademarks. Early consultation with trademark council is advised.

VI. THE INTELLECTUAL PROPERTY AUDIT

Before embarking in an extensive and expensive program designed to create and distribute programs to distance learning centers, an intellectual property audit should be performed. This involves organizing the primary written and video material you intend to exploit and all pertinent agreements covering rights to these works. Oral understandings should be set down in writing and questions of ownership and rights to exploit materials resolved. As new works are created, written agreements should delineate the ownership and use entitlement. All trademarks and service marks to be used should be protected and the most important ones registered with the U.S. period and foreign government trademark offices as appropriate. On an ongoing basis, the material that is created and used in the program should be properly archived and registered with the U.S. Copyright Office.

---

5   Starting in 1989, the Trademark Law was amended to permit filing of applications based on a bona fide "intent to use" ("ITU") a trademark. Once the mark is actually used, the ITU may be converted to a use-based registration, with protection dating back to the filing date of the ITU.

6   Many universities have established lucrative licensing programs built around their registered trademarks. Although the registration of trademarks or service marks related to "distance learning" may not yield similar revenue, registration will prevent others from "approaching" the goodwill inherent in a telecommunications organization's or university's trademark.

Northwest Michigan College

VII. CONCLUSION

The marriage of new technology and traditional teaching methods creates unique opportunities and challenges for entities involved in distance learning. One of the biggest challenges for telecommuncations organizations and participating universities will be to order their relationships with instructors and other contributors to protect themselves against charges of copyright infringement; at the same time, these entities must protect their works against copyright and trademark infringement by others.

Telecommunications organizations and participating universities should prepare a copyright audit to determine which materials they will incorporate into their programs, which rights have been secured and, most importantly, which remains to be secured. Organizations must assess these rights on a case-by-case basis. Written consents are the best means of ordering the rights between all involved parties; absent such agreements, the courts will order the relationships in a manner that may or may not be satisfactory to the telecommunications organization or the participating university. As the educational and commercial value of distance learning becomes more apparent, the need for clearly ordered copyright relationships will become equally obvious.

Finally, distance learning should be viewed as one important aspect of the emerging electronic superhighway. It is predictable that impressive technological advances will lead to policy initiatives, addressing practical and legal questions vital to educators. Now is the time to marshall resources and participate in the debate which will shape how effectively distance learning institutions will function in the 21st century.

For more information please contact
Kenneth D. Salomon at (202) 857-2566.

Copyright & Fair Use

M U S I C Materials

Learning Resource Services

Austin Community College

Illustrative Examples

(These examples are taken from The Copyright Primer and are used here with permission).

Question 1: Can the choral director make a new arrangement of a popular song and make photocopies for the college choir?
Answer: No. Under the guidelines, the fundamental character of the underlying work has been changed.

Question 2: The band owns sheet music for "I'm a Yankee Doodle Dandy." May the chorus director make photocopies so that the band and chorus may perform together at a college assembly?
Answer: No. Unless the situation is considered to be an emergency, no photo-copies can be made for a public performance.

Question 3: May a music appreciation teacher photocopy the first movement of a modern symphony for an exam question?
Answer: No. Under the guidelines, photocopying a performable unit is not permitted.

Question 4: May a teacher record a student's performance of copyrighted music?
Answer: Yes, but only for evaluation purposes. Multiple copies may not ordinarily be made.

WORKS CONSULTED

Crews, Kenneth D. Copyright, Fair Use, and the Challenge for Universities: Promoting the Progress of Higher Education. Chicago: University of Chicago Press, 1993.

Harper, Georgia. Copyright & the University Community. Austin: University of Texas System, 1993.

Helm, Virginia M. What Educators Should Know About Copyright. Bloomington, IN: Phi Delta Kappa Educational Foundation, 1986.

Reed, Mary Hutchings. The Copyright Primer. Chicago: Chicago Press Corporation, 1988.

United States. Copyright Office. Circular 21 Reproduction of Copyrighted Works by Educators and Librarians. Washington: GPO, 1991.

Vlcek, Charles W. Copyright Policy Development: A Resource Book for Educators. Friday Harbor, WA: Copyright Information Services, 1987.

Austin Community College

PREFACE

Please remember that the user who wants to duplicate copyrighted works always has the option of contacting the copyright owner for permission to copy. Often, the copyright owner will grant such permission either for a fee or without a fee.

Though there continues to be controversy regarding interpretation of the Copyright Law, this statement represents an effort to operate legally and to provide employees with guidelines that discourage violation of the law.

1. Employees of Austin Community College shall adhere to the provisions of the U.S. Copyright Law (Title 17, United States Code, Sect. 101, et. seq.).

2. Employees are prohibited from copying materials not specifically allowed by (1) the copyright law, (2) fair use guidelines, or (3) licenses or contractual agreements.

3. Austin Community College disapproves of unauthorized duplication in any form. Employees who willfully disregard these guidelines do so at their own risk and assume all liability.

4. College staff shall place appropriate copyright notices on or near all equipment capable of duplicating copyrighted materials.

5. Austin Community College shall keep current copyright guidelines designed to inform employees of their rights and responsibilities under the copyright law. Specific inquiries concerning copyright issues should be addressed to a campus Instructional Technology Manager or Head Librarian, or to the Dean of Learning Resource Services.

(For a discussion of the doctrine of fair use, see the brochure entitled "Copyright and Fair Use - Print Materials.")

COPYING MUSIC

The following guidelines may be found in Circular 21 Reproduction of Copyrighted Works by Educators and Librarians, p. 11-12. They were developed by representatives of the Music Publishers' Association of the United States, Inc., the National Music Publishers' Association, Inc., the Music Teachers National Association, the Music Educators National Conference, the National Association of School of Music, and the Ad Hoc Committee on Copyright Law Revision.

The following uses are permissible:

1. Emergency copying to replace purchased copies which are not available for an imminent performance, provided that purchased replacement copies shall be substituted in due course.

2. For academic purposes other than performance, single or multiple copies of excerpts of works may be made, provided that the excerpts do not comprise a part of the whole which would constitute a performable unit such as a section, movement, or aria, but in no case more than 10 percent of the whole work. The number of copies shall not exceed one copy per pupil.

3. Printed copies which have been purchased may be edited or simplified provided that the fundamental character of the work is not distorted or the lyrics, if any, altered or lyrics added if none exist.

4. A single copy of a sound recording (such as a tape, disc, or cassette) of performances by students may be made for evaluation or rehearsal purposes and may be retained by the educational institution or individual teacher.

5. A single copy of a sound recording (such as a tape, disc or cassette) of copyrighted music may be made from sound recordings owned by an educational institution or an individual teacher for the purpose of constructing aural exercises or examinations and may be retained by the educational institution or individual teacher.

The following uses are prohibited:

6. Copying to create a substitute or replacement for anthologies, compilations or collective works.

7. Copying of or from works intended to be "consumable" in the course of study or of teaching such as workbooks, exercises, and standardized tests and answer sheets and like material.

8. Copying for the purpose of performance, except as in (1) above.

9. Copying for the purpose of substituting for the purchase of music, except as in (1) and (2) above.

10. Copying without inclusion of the copyright notice which appears on the printed copy.

Software Materials

Copyright & Fair Use

Learning Resource Services

Austin Community College

---

subject to copyright laws and such copying is not permitted. The computers should have notices that inform users of copyright laws.

Question 4: An instructor has purchased software for use on his office computer. May he install the same software on his home computer?

Answer: Probably not. Most software license agreements permit installation on a single computer. Even if the organization has a site license, allowing for use on several computers, use of the software on a home computer would not be permissible because it is off site. Some software vendors, however, do allow this type of use, so be sure to carefully read the license agreement.

Copying Digital Media

Recent innovations in computer and information technologies such as high quality graphic scanners, CD-ROMs, high speed modems, Internet, etc. have made access to and retrieval of all types of media very easy. However, just because these media are easily accessible an stored in digital format does not mean that they are not copyright protected! While there is still much debate on how existing copyright laws apply to these types of media, they should be treated the same as traditional media with regard to copyright and fair use.

--- Works Consulted ---

Crews, Kenneth D. *Copyright, fair use, and the challenge for Universities: promoting the progress of higher education.* Chicago: University of Chicago Press, 1993.

Harper, Georgia. *Copyright & the university community.* Austin: University of Texas System, 1993.

Helm, Virginia M. *What educators should know about copyright.* Bloomington, IN: Phi Delta Kappa Educational Foundation, 1986.

Reed, Mary Hutchings. *The copyright primer.* Chicago: Chicago Press Corporation, 1988.

Software Publishers Assocation. *Software use and the law.* Washington, DC: Software Publisers Association, 1992.

Vlcek, Charles W. *Copyright policy development: a resource book for educators.* Friday Harbor, WA: Copyright Information Services, 1987.

© Austin Community College Fall '94

PREFACE

Please remember that the user who wants to duplicate copyrighted works always has the option of contacting the copyright owner for permission to copy. Often, the copyright owner will grant such permission either for a fee or without a fee.

Though there continues to be controversy regarding interpretation of the Copyright Law, this statement represents an effort to operate legally and to provide employees with guidelines that discourage violation of the law.

1. Employees of Austin Community College shall adhere to the provisions of the U.S. Copyright Law (Title 17, United States Code, Sect. 101, et. seq.).

2. Employees are prohibited from copying materials not specifically allowed by (1) the copyright law, (2) fair use guidelines, or (3) licenses or contractual agreements.

3. Austin Community College disapproves of unauthorized duplication in any form. Employees who willfully disregard these guidelines do so at their own risk and assume all liability.

4. College staff shall place appropriate copyright notices on or near all equipment capable of duplicating copyrighted materials.

5. Austin Community College shall keep current copyright guidelines designed to inform employees of their rights and responsibilities under the copyright law. Specific inquiries concerning copyright issues should be addressed to a campus Instructional Technology Manager or Head Librarian, or to the Dean of Learning Resource Services.

(For a discussion of the doctrine of fair use, see the brochure entitled "Copyright and Fair Use - Print Materials.")

Copying Computer Software

Anyone who purchases a computer program has the right to load the program onto a *single* computer and to make *another* copy "for archival purposes only." The license agreement included with the program *may* give the user additional rights, therefore, the agreement should be read carefully.

Because a copyright symbol or statement of copyright ownership is not required by law as a condition of protection, one cannot assume that the absence of such a notice implies permission to copy the software. Some types of computer software have less stringent rules on copying. These types include shareware, freeware and public domain software.

Shareware. This type of software is try-before-you-buy software and may be copied from bulletin boards or another user's disk. Each program comes with a license agreement that specifies how long it may be retained before it must be purchased. Shareware is registered with the author or publisher by sending a fee which varies according to each shareware program's license agreement. Registering the program entitles the user to continue using the program and to receive technical support, printed documentation, bug fixes and new version updates.

Freeware. This type of software is copyrighted but can be freely copied and distributed. The copyright protection usually restricts users from selling or distributing the software for profit, altering or reverse engineering the program, or claiming the program as their own. You do not have to register freeware.

Public Domain. This type of software may or may not be copyrighted, and it may or may not have a listed author. Public domain means that the software costs nothing to keep and use and that it is freely distributed to the public. The main difference between public domain software and freeware is that usually there is no way to contact the author, and most likely there will be no support of any kind available for the software.

Because it if often difficult to determine whether software is in the public domain or copyrighted and, if copyrighted, whether it is shareware or freeware, the following suggestions may help users stay within the laws regarding copyright:

a. Assume all software is copyrighted even if it does not bear a copyright symbol. The only source for permission to copy copyrighted software is either a specific grant of that right in a license agreement or the express or implied (with regard to freeware) permission of the copyright holder.

b. Retain all packaging materials that contain provisions of a licensing agreement between the user and the software copyright holder. Refer to these materials for information about what copying is permissible for the particular software program. Note that most license agreements prohibit renting, leasing or lending original copies of software.

Examples

Question 1: An instructor makes several copies of a copyrighted computer program for students to use in the computer lab or at home.
Answer: This is prohibited by copyright laws and almost all license agreements.

Question 2: A computer center owns one copy of a program and two students want to use the program. May the lab technician install two copies of the program for student use?
Answer: Probably not, since most license agreements permit installing a program on a single computer at the same time.

Question 3: A computer center technician learns that a student is copying copyrighted software on the center's computers.
Answer: The technician should inform the student that the software is

Austin Community College

ADMINISTRATIVE PROCEDURES

Title: COPYRIGHT LAW COMPLIANCE: COMPUTER SOFTWARE AND APPLICATION	**Identification:** 3.511 **Page:** 1 of 4 **Effective Date:** December 9, 1993
Authority: SBE 6A-14.0262; 6A-14.0247 FS 240.319	**Signature/Approval:**

PURPOSE

The purpose of this administrative procedure is to establish procedural guidelines regarding the duplication and use of computer software.

PROCEDURE

Computer software is an intellectual product. Educational institutions are not exempt from the copyright laws.

Copyright law includes data, programs, documentation, and databases; each may be copyrighted separately: the data may be copyrighted as a compilation, or a collective work, and/or each item may be protected; the database software and the documentation (printed material) are copyrighted separately.

Section 101 defines a computer program as "a set of statements or instructions to be used directly or indirectly in a computer in order to bring about a certain result." Computer programs are protected under the 1976 Copyright Act and are classed and registered as literary works. Both the source code and the object code are protected on the same copyright registration form because the codes are considered by the U.S. Copyright office as two representations of the same computer program.

Using the definition for "copies" found in Section 101 of the Copyright Act, a person using a copyrighted computer program is making a copy every time the program is loaded into memory.

"Copies are material objects, other than phonorecords, in which a work is fixed by any method now known or later developed, and from which the work can be perceived, reproduced, or otherwise communicated, either directly or with the aid of a machine or device."

Section 117 of the 1976 Copyright Act, amended in 1980, allows copying or adapting a computer program only where use of the computer itself cannot be achieved unless the program is loaded into the machine and a copy made, or the copy is made for archival purposes.

ADMINISTRATIVE PROCEDURES

Identification:	Page:	Effective Date:
3.511	2 of 4	December 9, 1993

It is now considered a felony to duplicate or distribute software or its documentation without the permission of the copyright owner.

1. <u>DUPLICATION OF SOFTWARE</u> - The Copyright Act (Title 17, <u>U.S. Code</u>, Sects. 101, 103, and 117) authorizes making one backup or archival copy of a program which is legally owned;

    A. Only software legally purchased by the institution may be used on HCC computers.

    B. Only employees and students of HCC may use HCC-owned software and hardware.

    C. The copy made must not be used as a second copy. The copy must be destroyed if the continued possession of the computer program ceases to be rightful.

    D. HCC-owned software must be used exclusively on HCC hardware and may not be copied for use at home.

    E. The individual employee is responsible for the legal use of software on hardware assigned to him/her. In a laboratory situation, the employee responsible for the lab is responsible for the legal use of software on the hardware located in the lab.

    F. The Software Rental Amendments Act of 1990 (PL 101-650) prohibits the rental, leasing, or lending of original copies of any software without permission.

    G. Written copies of permissions and licenses should be kept on file in the employee's work area or in the lab, as appropriate.

2. <u>CONVERTING AND TRANSFERRING</u> - Changing a copyrighted work from one format to another is considered creating a derivative work and is a right of the copyright owner. Persons may maintain both a 5¼" and a 3.5" format copy since only one archival copy is permitted. It is recommended that permission be requested to make this change.

    Similarly, if the content of a floppy disk (5¼") or a microdisk (3.5") is transferred to a hard disk, the disk must become the archive copy.

Hillsborough Community College

ADMINISTRATIVE PROCEDURES

Identification: 3.511	Page: 3 of 4	Effective Date: December 9, 1993

Multiple loading of programs into several machines constitutes making multiple copies which is not permitted under the law unless a multi-use license has been obtained.

3. NETWORKING AND MULTIPLE MACHINE LOADING - Although there are no specific guidelines written into law related to networking, the consensus of legal opinion indicates the strong possibility of infringement in the area of fair use. The purpose of use and the impact on the marketing of the copyright owner's materials must be considered.

Therefore, HCC subscribes to the 1980 Computer Software Act:

Networking other computers or terminals to one hard disk is an infringement unless a networking license is obtained for each copyrighted software placed on the hard disk.

Multiple loading of programs into several machines constitutes making multiple copies which is not permitted under the law.

4. DATABASES

A. Downloading

Online databases are protected by copyright law; downloading is the process of transferring information found online to a microcomputer printer, or hard drive in order to use the information. Regulations for accessing and downloading a specific database are usually defined in a vendor contract.

There are no exemptions for educational institutions or libraries.

Employees and students are advised to follow these guidelines:

(1) review all contracts or license agreements.

(2) do not retain archival copies of a downloaded search.

(3) do not use the downloaded material to create a derivative work.

(4) inform all library and lab users of the conditions of the databases they search.

Hillsborough Community College

ADMINISTRATIVE PROCEDURES

B.   Creating and Distributing

The Fair Use Guidelines pertain only to print material, not to computer databases. In terms of public display, the exemption for a performance is not met because the instructor is not present and the information is not necessarily related to the curriculum. In attempting to develop a database from copyrighted material, the employee or student must secure permission from the author for the right to copy the material into a database and to distribute the databases though multiple copies or multi-terminal viewing.

2.12

RESPONSIBLE USE OF INFORMATION TECHNOLOGY

In pursuit of its mission of teaching, educational excellence, and public service, the Board of Trustees of Kirkwood Community College provides access to computing and information resources for faculty, staff, students, and other authorized users within institutional priorities and financial capabilities.

All members of the College community who use Kirkwood's computing resources are responsible for the integrity of the resources. All users of College-owned or College-leased information technology systems must respect the integrity of the physical facilities and controls, and comply with all pertinent licenses and controls. In addition, users and system administrators will respect the privacy of person-to-person communications in all forms, including voice (telephone and voice mail boxes), text (electronic mail and file transfer), and image (graphics and television). The principles of academic freedom will apply to public communications in all of these forms.

College Information Technology facilities and accounts are to be used for College related activities for which they are intended and authorized. The College reserves the right to extend, limit, restrict, or deny computing privileges and access to its information resources. Procedures, enforcement, and responsibilities are outlined in <u>the Policy for Responsible Use of Information Technology</u> that was adopted by the Instructional Technology Committee, December, 1995.

TABLE OF CONTENTS

POLICY FOR RESPONSIBLE USE OF INFORMATION TECHNOLOGY
AT KIRKWOOD COMMUNITY COLLEGE

In pursuit of its mission of teaching, educational excellence, and public service, the Board of Trustees of Kirkwood Community College provides access to computing and information resources for students, faculty, staff, and other authorized users within institutional priorities and financial capabilities.

The Policy for Responsible Use of Information Technology at Kirkwood contains the governing philosophy for regulating faculty, student, staff and other authorized users of the College's information technology resources.   This policy establishes the general principles regarding appropriate use of equipment, software, and networks.   By adopting this policy, the College recognizes that all members of the College are also bound by local, state, and federal laws relating to copyrights, security, and other statutes regarding electronic media

Policy

All members of the College community who use Kirkwood's computing are responsible for the integrity of the resources.   All users of College-owned or College-leased information technology systems must respect the rights of other users, respect the integrity of the physical facilities and controls, and comply with all pertinent licenses and contractual agreements.   Kirkwood's policy requires that all members of its community act within relevant laws and contractual obligations, and the highest standard of ethics.

Users and system administrators will respect the privacy of person-to-person communications in all forms, including voice (telephone) voice mail boxes, text (electronic mail and file transfer), and image (graphics and television).   The principle of academic freedom will apply to public communications in all these forms.

Access to the College's Information Technology facilities and resources is a privilege granted to College students, faculty, and staff.   Access to College information resources may be granted by the owners of that information based on the owner's judgment of the following factors: relevant laws and contractual obligations, the

1

requester's need to know, the information sensitivity, and the risk of damage to or loss by the College.

The College reserves the right to extend, limit, restrict, or deny computing privileges and access to its information resources. Data owners--whether departments, units, faculty, students, or staff-- may allow individuals other than College faculty, staff, and students access to information for which they are responsible, so long as such access does not violate any license or contractual agreement; College policy; or any federal, state, county, or local law or ordinance, and so long as such access does not negatively impact primary users.

College Information Technology facilities and accounts are to be used for the College-related activities for which they are intended and authorized. College Information Technology resources are not to be used for commercial purposes or non-College related activities without written authorization from the College. In these cases the College will require payment of appropriate fees. This policy applies equally to all College-owned or College-leased computers and peripherals. Similarly, solicitation for any purpose also requires written authorization from the college.

Access to information resources without proper authorization from the data owner, unauthorized use of College computing facilities, and intentional corruption or misuse of information resources are direct violations of the College's standards for conduct.

Enforcement

Alleged violations of this policy shall be handled according to the judicial processes outlined in the Kirkwood Community College Personnel Policies and Procedures Manual, College collective bargaining agreements, the Student Code of Conduct, the Code of Academic Integrity. Kirkwood treats access and use violations of computing facilities, equipment, software, information resources, networks, or privileges seriously. Kirkwood will pursue criminal and civil prosecution of violators as deemed necessary.

PROCEDURES & GUIDELINES

User Responsibilities

If you use the College's information technology resources or facilities, you have the following responsibilities:

* To use the College's information technology facilities and information resources, including hardware, software, networks, and computer accounts, responsibly and appropriately, respecting the rights of other information technology users and respecting all contractual and license agreements. The software made available by the College has been licensed by the College for your use. As a result, its use may be subject to certain limitations.

* To use only those computers and computer accounts for which you have authorization.

* To use only those voice mail boxes and telephone account codes for which you are authorized.

* To use network accounts only for the purpose(s) for which they have been issued. Use College owned microcomputers and advanced workstations for College related projects only.

* To be responsible for the use of all your accounts and for protecting each account's password. Do not share computer accounts. **WARNING:** The sharing of passwords constitutes the greatest threat to network integrity. Do not share your password. If you suspect a violation, change your password.

* To promptly report unauthorized use of your accounts to your project director, instructor, supervisor, system administrator or other appropriate College authority.

* To cooperate with system administrator requests for information about computing or information technology activities or both. Under certain unusual circumstances, a system administrator is authorized to access your files (e.g. for reasons of system integrity/protection), except voice mail

3

boxes which are not accessible by the system administrator without changing the password first.

* To take reasonable and appropriate steps to see that all hardware and software license agreements are faithfully executed on any system, network or server that you operate.

Each user is ultimately responsible for his or her own computing and his or her own work using information technology resources. For example, users should remember to make backup copies of their data, files, programs, diskettes and tapes, particularly those created on microcomputers and those used on individually- or departmentally-operated systems. Furthermore, users with desktop computers or other computers they operate themselves must remember they may be acting in the same capacity with the same responsibilities as the system administrators for those computers and need to take that responsibility very seriously.

If you are a project director for a group of network computing users, a supervisor whose staff use computers, or a faculty member whose students use computers, you must help your project members, staff, or students learn more about ethical computing practices. You should also help your project members, staff, or students learn about good information technology practices and data management.

Password Security

Passwords still form the most common method by which outsiders penetrate an account. The following guidelines will help minimize the possibility of anyone discovering your password and gaining access to your account privileges:

a. Do not give your password to any other individual.
b. Do not type your password while someone is watching you work.
c. Change your password frequently. The password system may be installed to force periodic changes for you.
d. Avoid passwords that reference personal data for you, your friends, or family (names, birthdates, etc.).
e. Avoid using words that are contained in the dictionary or that are popular in this environment.

f. Use passwords that have lower and upper case letters, as well as numbers or other special characters.
g. Here are some examples of some easy to remember but hard to guess passwords:

    1. asits9   (a stitch in time saves nine)
    2. girLfriend (capitalize one letter)
    3. bilker   (add strange punctuation to a word)

h. Do not post or announce your password in publicly accessible areas.
i. When changing your password, avoid using the old password plus one additional character or digit.

System Administrator Responsibilities

This document uses the phrase system administrator to refer to all of the following College personnel:

* Staff employed by a central computing office such as the Computer Information Systems whose responsibilities include system, site, or network administration.

* Staff employed by other College departments whose duties include system, site, or network administration.

A system administrator's use of the College's computing resources is governed by the same guidelines as any other user's. However, a system administrator has additional responsibilities to the users of the network, site, system, or systems he or she administers:

* A system administrator manages systems, networks, and servers to provide available software and hardware to users for their College computing and information technology needs.

* A system administrator is responsible for both the physical security and access protection of a system, network, or server.

* A system administrator must take reasonable and appropriate steps to see that all hardware and software license agreements are faithfully executed on all systems, networks, and servers for which he or she has responsibility.

* A system administrator must take reasonable precautions to guard against corruption of data or software or damage to hardware or facilities. The College is not responsible for loss of information from misuse, malfunction of hardware, malfunction of software, or external contamination of data or programs. The staff in central units such as the office of Computer Information Systems and all other system administrators must make every effort to ensure the integrity of the College's information technology systems and the information stored thereon. However, users must be aware that no security or back-up system is 100% effective.

* A system administrator must treat information about and information stored by the system's user as confidential.

As an aid to a better understanding of responsible computing practices, all departments that own or lease computing or information technology equipment are encouraged to develop "Conditions of Use" or "Guidelines for Responsible Use of Information Technology" documentation for all systems that they operate and to make these documents available to users. These documents must be consistent with the "Policy for Responsible Use of Information Technology at Kirkwood Community College" (reprinted on pages 1 & 2 of these guidelines) and should be approved by the department's administrative officer or an individual designated by that administrative officer.

College Responsibilities

Access to the College's Information Technology facilities is a privilege granted to College students, faculty, and staff. Access to College information resources may be granted by the owners of that information based on the owner's judgment of the following factors: relevant laws and contractual obligations, the requester's need to know, the information's sensitivity, and the risk of damage to or loss by the College.

The College reserves the right to extend, limit, restrict, or deny computing privileges and access to its information resources. The College will maintain the computing resources in good operating condition, providing timely repair and installation when needed. The College will also be responsible for the following activities relating to access to information resources:

* provide adequate security measures to protect the College's information resources.

* provide access to documentation (manuals and information files) pertaining to the College's information resources.

* provide education and training for users of the College's information technology resources through formal training sessions or system messages.

* prominently display messages in computer labs about user's responsibilities.

* provide and maintain access to resources outside the campus through traditional telecommunication methods.

The College recognizes five classes of users of the College's information resources.

1. Kirkwood employees (staff, faculty, or administrator).
2. Kirkwood students enrolled in a class that requires the use of computing resources.
3. Kirkwood students not enrolled in a class that requires the use of computing resources but who desire such use.
4. District residents contracting use of computing resources.(fee based)
5. A company renting Kirkwood computing resources.

The College will ensure that each class of user has been notified of its responsibilities and maintain an active list of users. The College will require each user to request access to information services by submitting the appropriate request form.

7

Misuse of Information Technology and Information Resource Privileges

The College characterizes misuse of information technology and information resources privileges as unethical and unacceptable and as just cause for taking disciplinary action. Misuse of information technology and information resource privileges includes, but is not restricted to, the following:

* attempting to modify or remove computer equipment or other equipment supporting information technology, software, or peripherals without proper authorization.

* accessing computers, other equipment supporting information technology, computer software, computer data or information, or networks without proper authorization, regardless of whether the computer, software, data information, or network in question is owned by the College. (That is, if you abuse the networks to which the College belongs or the computers at other sites connected to those networks, the College will treat this matter as an abuse of your Kirkwood computing privileges.)

* circumventing or attempting to circumvent normal resource limits, logon procedures, and security regulations.

* using computing facilities, computer accounts, computer data, or other information resources for purposes other than those for which they were intended or authorized.

* using College Information Technology resources for commercial purposes or non-College related activities without written authorization from the College.

* sending fraudulent computer mail, breaking into another user's electronic mailbox, or voice mailbox, or reading someone else's electronic mail without his or her permission.

* sending any fraudulent electronic transmission, including but not limited to fraudulent requests for confidential information, fraudulent submission of electronic purchase

8

requisitions or journal vouchers, and fraudulent electronic authorization or purchase requisitions or journal vouchers.

* violating any software license agreement or copyright, including copying or redistributing copyrighted computer software, data, or reports without proper, recorded authorization.

* violating the property rights of copyright holders who are in possession of computer generated data, reports, or software.

* using the College's computing resources, voice mailboxes and telephones to harass or threaten other users.

* taking advantage of another user's naivete or negligence to gain access to any computer account, telephone account, data, software, or file that is not your own and for which you have not received explicit authorization to access.

* physically interfering with other users' access to the College's computing facilities.

* encroaching on others' use of the College's computers (e.g. disrupting others' computer use by excessive game playing; sending frivolous or excessive messages, either locally or off-campus (including electronic chain letters and unauthorized electronic "bulk" mailings); printing excess copies of documents, files, data, or programs; modifying system facilities, operating systems, or disk partitions; attempting to crash or tie up a College computer; damaging or vandalizing College computing facilities, equipment, software, or computer files) attempting to degrade system performance or capability.

* using accounts assigned for another's exclusive use.

* using Kirkwood's computing resources to copy, generate or transmit obscene materials, or making obscene files publicly accessible.

9

* disclosing or removing proprietary information, software, printed output or magnetic media without the explicit permission of the owner.

* posting credit card numbers or passwords in publicly accessible locations on computer systems.

* reading other users' data, information, files, or programs on a display screen, as printed output, or via electronic means, without the owner's explicit permission.

User Confidentiality and System Integrity

The College will keep automatic logs of user activity for accounting, allocation of resources and facility utilization, however, the College will not normally monitor individual usage of any general facility. The College reserves the right to monitor and record the usage of all facilities if threatening or abusive behavior has been reported. The College has the right to use information gained in this way in disciplinary or criminal proceedings, as permitted by Federal and State law.

Address Inspection of User Files

If a system administrator is an eyewitness to an information technology abuse; notices an unusual degradation of service or other aberrant behavior on the system, network, or server for which he or she is responsible; or receives a complaint of computing abuse or degradation of service, he or she should investigate and take steps to maintain the integrity of the system(s). If a system administrator has evidence that leads to a suspicion that a user's computing activity is the probable source of a problem or of abuse, he or she must weigh the potential danger to the system and its users against the confidentiality of that user's information.

While investigating a suspected abuse of information technology; a suspected hardware failure; a disruption of service; or a suspected bug in an application program, compiler, network, operating system, or system utility, a system administrator should ordinarily ask a user's permission before inspecting that user's files, diskettes, or tapes. The next two paragraphs outline exceptions to this rule.

If in the best judgment of the system administrator, the action of one user threatens other users or if a system or network for which the system administrator is responsible is in grave, imminent danger of crashing, sustaining damage to its hardware or software, or sustaining damage to user jobs, the system administrator should act quickly to protect the system and its users. In the event that he or she has had to inspect user files in the pursuit of this important responsibility, he or she must notify, as soon as possible his or her own administrative officer or other individual designated by that administrative officer of his or her action and the reasons for taking that action. Documentation of the action and the reasons for taking such action should be completed as quickly as reasonable. The administrative officer or his or her designee needs must notify one of the following: the user or users whose files were inspected; the user's instructor, supervisor, project director, or administrative officer.

In cases in which the user is not available in a timely fashion, in which the user is suspected of malicious intent to damage a computer system, or in which notifying the user would impede a sensitive investigation of serious computer abuse, the system administrator may inspect the information in question so long as he notifies his or her own administrative officer or other individual designated by the administrative officer of his or her actions and the reasons for taking those actions. The administrative officer needs to be certain that the user's instructor, supervisor, project director, or administrative officer, is notified of the situation. In the case of suspected malicious intent, the administrative officer may also need to refer the matter to the appropriate College disciplinary body or the Department of Public Safety.

A system administrator may find it necessary to suspend or restrict a user's computing privileges or use of other Information Technology during the investigation of a problem. The system administrator should confer with his or her administrative officer or other person designated by that administrative officer before taking this step. A user may appeal such a suspension or restriction and petition for reinstatement of computing privileges, or use of Information Technology through appropriate grievance procedures.

11

In general, then, a system administrator should:

* protect the integrity of the system entrusted to his or her care

* respect the confidentiality of the information users have stored on the system

* notify appropriate individuals when the above two aims have come into conflict

* assist his or her administrative officer in referring cases of suspected abuse to the appropriate College disciplinary process.

Process for Cases of Alleged Misuse of Computing and Information Resource Privileges and Penalties for Misuse of Computing and Information Resource Privileges

If system administrators have evidence of intentional or malicious misuse of computing activities or the computer files of an individual, the system administrators have the obligation to pursue any or all of the following steps to protect the user community:

* Take action to protect the system(s), a user's computer jobs, and a user's files from damage. Notify the alleged abuser's instructor, supervisor, project director, or administrative officer of the investigation.

* Refer the matter for further inquiry to the appropriate College disciplinary system. If necessary, staff members from the offices Telecommunications, Instructional Technology or Information Systems as well as faculty or staff members with technology expertise may be called upon to advise the College on the implications of the evidence presented and of the seriousness of the offense.

* Suspend or restrict the alleged abuser's computing and information technology privileges during the inquiry. A user may appeal such a suspension or restriction and petition for reinstatement of computing privileges through appropriate grievance procedures.

12

* Inspect the alleged abuser's files, diskettes, and/or tapes. System administrators must be certain that the trail of evidence leads to the user's activities or computing files before inspecting any user's files. Documentation of the action and the reasons for taking such action should be completed as quickly as reasonable. (See "User Confidentiality and System Integrity" on page 8 of these Guidelines for more information.)

Ordinarily, the administrative officer whose department is responsible for the computing system on which the alleged misuse occurred should refer the matter for further inquiry to the appropriate College disciplinary system. As the case develops, other administrative offices including Public Safety may assume part of the responsibility for prosecuting the case.

Abuse of computing privileges may be subject to disciplinary action. Disciplinary action may include the loss of computing privileges and other disciplinary sanctions up to and including discharge, and/or dismissal. In all cases appropriate procedures will be followed and due process respected. An abuser of the College's computing resources may also be liable for civil or criminal prosecution.

It should be understood that nothing in these guidelines precludes enforcement under the laws and regulations of the State of Iowa, any municipality or county therein, and/or United States of America. Similarly, nothing in these guidelines should be construed as a contract that diminishes constitutional rights to free speech and privacy.

Academic Integrity

Faculty and students are reminded that computer-assisted plagiarism is still plagiarism. All of the following uses of a computer are violations of the College's guidelines for academic integrity and are punishable as acts of plagiarism:

* copying a computer file that contains someone else's work and submitting it as one's own work.

13

* copying a computer file that contains someone else's work and using it as a model for one's own work without proper acknowledgement.

* working together on an assignment, sharing the computer files or programs involved, and then submitting individual copies of the assignment as one's own individual work.

* knowingly allowing a student to copy or use one's own computer files and to submit those files, or an unacknowledged modification thereof, as his or her individual work.

For further information on this topic, students are urged to consult the Kirkwood Community College Code of Academic Integrity, or to consult with their individual instructors. Faculty members are urged to develop specific class related guidelines regarding academic integrity and to communicate those guidelines to their students in writing.

14

DEFINITION OF TERMS

Administrative Officer: vice-president, executive director, dean, director, or manager to whom an individual reports.

Authorized User: someone who makes use of a computer system or network but who does not necessarily have system administrator responsibilities for that computer system or network. A user is responsible for his or her use of the computer and/or the network and for learning proper data management strategies.

Computer Account: the combination of a user number, user name, or user ID and a password that allows an individual access to a network computer.

Data Owner: the individuals or department that can authorize access to information, data, or software and is responsible for the integrity and accuracy of that information, data, or software. Specifically, the data owner can be the author of the information, data, or software or can be the individual or department that has negotiated a license for the College's use of the information, data, or software.

Desktop Computers, Microcomputers, Advanced Workstations: different classes of smaller computers, some shared, some single-user systems. If owned, or leased by the College or if owned by an individual and connected to a College-owned, leased, or operated network, use of these computers is covered by the Kirkwood Policy for Responsible Use of Information Technology.

Information Resources: data or information and the software and hardware that makes that data or information available to users. Telephone systems, voice mail systems, television (distance learning) systems.

Information Technology: the processing of voice, data, images, and text. This includes the acquisition, development, dissemination, protection, and storage of information through the use of technology and the installation and maintenance of the hardware/software to accomplish this.

15

Network: a group of telephones or computers and peripherals that share information electronically, typically connected to each other by either cable, satellite link, or other technologies.

Normal Resource Limits: the amount of disk space, memory, printing, etc. allocated to your computer account by that computer's system administrator.

Peripherals: an auxiliary device including, without limitation, a digital scanner, modem, camera, printer, fax machine or telephone handset, that works in conjunction with the information technology facilities and resources.

Project Director: person charged with administering a group of computer accounts and the computing resources used by the people using those computer accounts.

Software: programs, data or information stored on magnetic media (tapes, disks, diskettes, cassettes, etc.) usually used to refer to computer programs.

System Administrator: staff employed by a central computing department such as offices of Telecommunications, Instructional Technology or Computer Information Systems whose responsibilities include system, site, or network administration. System administrators perform functions including, but not limited to, installing hardware and software, managing a computer or network, and keeping Informational Resources computer operational.

Systems: see Information Technology facilities and resources.

Telephone Account Code: a combination of numbers that allows an individual access to a long distance call.

User: see Authorized User.

(Kirkwood is intellectually indebted to Oakton Community College and to the University of Cincinnati for considerable use of their Responsible Use Policy.)

Employee Access Request Form

Last Name_____First Name_____

Home Telephone Number (___)_____-_____

Work Telephone Number (___)_____-_____

Social Security Number ____-___-____

Department_____Administrator_____

Requested Login ID (min. of 5 characters, max. of 8 specify lower and uppercase)_____

Requested effective date of Login ID_____

KCC Network Access

Administrative Network	__Yes	__No
Academic Network	__Yes	__No
Unix Access	__Yes	__No
AS400 Access	__Yes	__No
Internet Access	__Yes	__No
Mainframe	__Yes	__No
Other(specify)_____	__Yes	__No

I have read the Policy and Procedures and Guidelines for the Responsible Use of Information Technology and agree to abide by their provisions. I understand that violation of the provisions stated may result in disciplinary action including the loss of computing privileges and other sanctions as provided in relevant contracts, policies and procedures.

Employee Signature_____Date_____

For Internal Use Only

KCC Network	Date Created	By Whom	Date Deleted	By Whom
Administrative	_____	_____	_____	_____
Academic	_____	_____	_____	_____
AS400	_____	_____	_____	_____
Unix	_____	_____	_____	_____
Internet	_____	_____	_____	_____
Mainframe	_____	_____	_____	_____
Other(specify)	_____	_____	_____	_____

17

Student Employee Access Request Form

Last Name _____First Name_____
Home Telephone Number (___)____-_____
Work Telephone Number (___)____-_____
Social Security Number _____-___-_____

Department____._____Administrator's signature_____

Requested Login ID (min. of 5 characters, max. of 8 specify lower
and uppercase)_____
Requested effective date of Login ID_____
Requested expiration date of Login ID_____

KCC Network Access
        Administrative Network   __Yes__No
        Academic Network   __Yes__No
Unix Access   __Yes__No
AS400 Access   __Yes__No
Internet Access   __Yes__No
Mainframe   __Yes__No
Other (specify)_____   __Yes__No

I have read the Policy and Procedures and Guidelines for the Responsible Use of
Information Technology and agree to abide by their provisions. I understand that
violation of the provisions stated may result in disciplinary action including
the loss of computing privileges and other disciplinary sanctions under the Code
of Student conduct including dismissal.

Student Employee Signature_____Date_____

For Internal Use Only

KCC Network	Date Created	By Whom	Date Deleted	By Whom
Administrative	_____	_____	_____	_____
Academic	_____	_____	_____	_____
AS400	_____	_____	_____	_____
Unix	_____	_____	_____	_____
Internet	_____	_____	_____	_____
Mainframe	_____	_____	_____	_____
Other (specify)	_____	_____	_____	_____

18

Kirkwood Community College

Student Access Request Form

Name_____

Home Telephone (____)____-_____
Work Telephone (____)____-_____
Social Security Number _____-___-_____

I have read the Policy and Procedures and Guidelines for the
Responsible Use of Information Technology and agree to abide by
their provisions. I understand that violation of the provisions
stated may result in disciplinary action including the loss of
computing privileges and other disciplinary sanctions under the
Code of Student Conduct including dismissal.

Student Signature_____Date_____
_____

If you are requesting Unix and/or Internet access, you must
complete the following.

Sponsoring Faculty Member_____

Requested Unix Login ID (min 5 characters, max. of 8 specify upper
and lower case)_____

I agree to inform the student(s) of their responsibilities
regarding their use of Kirkwood's Information Technology resources
as defined in the Policy and Procedures and Guidelines for the
Responsible Use of Information Technology and to notify them that I
will expect them to adhere to these responsibilities.

Faculty Signature_____Date_____

For Internal Use Only

	Date Created	By Whom
KCC Network	_____	_____
AS400	_____	_____
Unix	_____	_____
Internet	_____	_____
Other(specify)	_____	_____

19

Class Access Request Form

Course Code_____Section_____

Faculty Member_____

Home Telephone Number (___)____-_____

Work Telephone Number (____)____-_____

Attach a class roster. If Unix and/or Internet access is required, indicate the following information for each student. See the examples below.

Student SSN	Student Name	Unix Login ID	Internet Access(Y/N)
1.111-22-3333	Sally Fields	sfields	Y
2.222-33-4444	Bob I. Telnet	bobit	Y
3.333-44-5555	Gary Usenet	garyu	N

I agree to inform the student(s) of their responsibilities regarding their use of Kirkwood's Information Technology resources as defined in the Policy and Procedures and Guidelines for the Responsible Use of Information Technology and to notify them that I will expect them to adhere to these responsibilities.

Faculty Signature_____Date_____

For Internal Use Only

	Date Created	By Whom
KCC Network	_____	_____
AS400	_____	_____
Unix	_____	_____
Internet	_____	_____
Other(specify)	_____	_____

20

Kirkwood Community College

District Resident Access Request Form

Name_____

Address_____

City, State, Zip_____

Home Telephone Number (____)_____-_____

Work Telephone Number (____)_____-_____

KCC Network Requested Login ID (min. 5 characters, max of 8 specify upper and lower case)_____

I have read the Policy and Procedures and Guidelines for the Responsible Use of Information Technology and agree to abide by their provisions. I understand that violation of the provisions stated may result in disciplinary action, including the loss of computing privileges. Kirkwood will pursue criminal and civil prosecution of violators as necessary.

Signature_____Date_____

In addition to Policy and Procedures and Guidelines for the Responsible Use of Information Technology, here are other conditions that apply to district residents

1. There will be no refunds on the balance of your account.
2. Access to software will be limited to those applications which appear on the menu. Software will not and may not be loaded onto the network file servers or hard drives on any machines.
3. You are purchasing access to computers, printers and software on the campus where your ID is created.
4. The computers, printers and software will be available only during published operating hours.
5. You are limited to the licenses of the individual software packages.
6. Software is protected by copyright law. Copying software is in violation of Federal Law and College policies. Suspected violations will be vigorously investigated and, if warranted, appropriate penalties applied. Specifically, you do not have the right to:

    -make copies of software for yourself or others.
    -receive and use unauthorized copies of software.

For Internal Use Only

	Date Created	By Whom
KCC Network	_____	_____
AS400	_____	_____
Unix	_____	_____
Internet	_____	_____
Other(specify)	_____	_____

21

Kirkwood Community College

Pennsylvania College of Technology

Williamsport, Pennsylvania

Board Policy Statement

Title: __Copyright Rights__   No: __III 3.05.07__

Page: __1 of 2__

Date Approved:__3/84__
           Month/Year   Page Number of Board Minutes __1588__

Date Revised:_____   Page Number of Board Minutes _____

Policy

3.05.07   (1)   All property rights in books, teaching aids (including workbooks, laboratory manuals, transparencies, tapes, films, and similar items) developed by College Employee(s) shall belong to the Employee(s) who produced the same. These shall include materials produced by an Employee in conjunction with his or her regular assignment, released time, or extended paid-time projects. Subject to the College's joint property rights stated herein, such property rights shall include the right to publish for private profit and the right to copyright any book, manual, or printed material.

Prior to seeking copyright or commercial publication of materials produced by an Employee in conjunction with College employment, the Employee shall acknowledge, in writing, the terms of this policy by contacting the College Personnel Office.

(2)   The College shall have a joint property right in books and teaching aids developed by an Employee as part of a regular assignment, released or extended paid-time projects, or facilitated through approved access to College facilities and/or College support. The College's joint property right does not necessarily imply endorsement of concepts, ideas, product, etc., developed by the Employee, nor shall it be represented as such.

(3)   Until such time as the College has been reimbursed to the extent and amount that the College financially supported said project, as determined by the Dean of Administration, (via regular wages, released time, extended paid-time, or purchase of supplies and materials), the College's joint property right shall entitle the College:

    1.   To use or purchase said item regardless of copyrights thereon.

    2.   To receive seventy-five percent of initial royalties, commissions, or other pecuniary profits resulting from creation of said items.

Board Policy Statement (<u>continued</u>)

Title No.: <u>III 3.05.07</u>

Page No.: <u>2 of 2</u>

Policy (<u>continued</u>)

(4) Once reimbursement for such College financial support has been made, royalties, commissions, or pecuniary profit thereafter earned by the sale of said item to any purchaser thereof shall belong exclusively to the Employee(s).

(5) An Employee shall not realize a pecuniary gain from students of the College or from the College itself on any books and teaching aids required or recommended for his classes except for appropriate royalties, commissions, or profits from commercial or university presses or production companies but excluding subsidy (vanity) presses, duplicating or printing companies and self production. Any books or teaching aids authored, edited, invented, or produced by the Employee and published, printed, or produced by the Employee himself or through subsidy publishing or production shall be made available to the students or the College at cost. A faculty member shall be required to obtain prior written approval of his Division Director and Dean whenever he requires or recommends purchase by students of the College of Instructional materials or books in which he holds property rights.

(6) Provisions (1) through (5) listed above are subject to all current and future provisions of applicable state and federal regulations with respect to all items produced in projects funded infull or in part with state or federal funds, or through other funding sources, such as foundations, which may apply any such restrictions or stipulations.

APPENDICES

CJCLS SURVEY OF COPYRIGHT POLICIES AND PRACTICES

Name and Title: _____*80 respondents representing 26% return*_____

Library and Institution: _____

Phone: _____ FAX Number: _____

Internet Address: _____

Please place an "x" next to the appropriate response or responses for each question:

1. Number of full-time equivalent (FTE) students, as listed in HEGIS report:
    22% _17_ fewer than 1000   *8%* _6_ 5000 - 7000
    26% _21_ 1000 - 3000   *9%* _7_ 7000 - 10,000
    22% _17_ 3000 - 5000   *13%* _10_ more than 10,000

2. Number of full-time equivalent staff in your library/learning resources center (include professional, paraprofessional, and clerical, but do not include student assistants):
    26% _21_ fewer than 5   *13%* _10_ 15 - 25
    26% _21_ 5 - 10   *1%* _4_ 25 - 40
    18% _14_ 10 - 15   *9%* _8_ more than 40

    66%   *34%*
3. Does your institution have a formal written copyright policy? _53_ Yes _27_ No
    If not, please continue to question #4.

    A. If YES, does the copyright policy encompass copyright
        61% _40_ Institution wide
        17% _11_ Library/Learning Resources Department as a whole
        1% _4_ Specific services? *audiovisual, printing, computing*

    B. If YES, how was the copyright policy endorsed or adopted?
        14% _9_ Institution Attorney
        38% _25_ Board of Trustees Action
        .5% _2_ Faculty Senate Action
        24% _16_ Administrative Procedure
        21% _14_ Library/Learning Resources Procedure
        .5% _3_ Other *State Board, Faculty Handbook, follow copyright law*

4. Do you have separate written copyright procedures and/or forms for the following?
    43% _34_ Interlibrary loan and Document Delivery
    34% _27_ Library/Learning Resources Reserve
    32% _26_ Off-Air Video Copying
    21% _17_ Media Production/Adaptation

--Over please--

191

13% _10_ Music Performance Rights
25% _20_ Computer Software/Databases
25% _20_ Copy Center/Print Duplication
1% _5_ Publications Center/College Information Office
1% _6_ College Bookstore
1% _4_ Electronic Information Transmission, e.g. Internet
_____ Other_____

5. Who is designated in charge of institutional copyright issues?
  53% _42_ No one person holds the responsibility
  21% _17_ Director of Learning Resources
  .5% _2_ Vice President of Business Affairs
  .5% _3_ Copyright Committee
  1% _8_ Other *Dean Students,Instruction,Administration; Public*
      Information Officer; College Attorney; Media Services

6. How do your faculty and staff learn about copyright issues?
  50% _40_ Written informational booklet
  25% _20_ Forms
  31% _25_ Workshops
  21% _16_ News Stories
  15% _12_ Electronic/Internet Resources
  30% _24_ Other *Adm procedure, newsletter/memo,signs, informal*
      consultation,faculty handbook, journal articles, guidelines

CJCLS PLANS TO PUBLISH A COLLECTION OF MODEL COPYRIGHT POLICIES, PROCEDURES, AND FORMS. IF YOU ARE WILLING TO SHARE YOUR POLICIES, PROCEDURES, AND FORMS AS LISTED ABOVE, PLEASE MAIL THEM BACK WITH THIS SURVEY. IN ADDITION, IF YOU HAVE STAFF DEVELOPMENT MATERIALS RELATED TO COPYRIGHT THAT YOU WOULD BE WILLING TO SHARE, PLEASE ALSO MAIL THEM BACK WITH THIS SURVEY.

_____

Permission is granted to reproduce any or all of the accompanying policies, procedures, forms, or staff development materials, with proper attribution given to the contributing Library/Learning Resources Department. The copyright for the publication will be held by the American Library Association.

_____ _____ _____
Your Name   Title   Date

*Please return this survey and documents **no later than April 1, 1996,** to:*

Wanda Johnston
1525 SE 42nd Avenue
Ocala, FL 34471

We thank you for your participation in this project!

CONTRIBUTING INSTITUTIONS

Austin Community College
W. Lee Hisle
Assoc. VP, Learning Resources
1212 Rio Grande Avenue
Austin, TX 78701
(512) 223-3069

Broome Community College
Charles Quagliata
Vice President of Community Affairs
Box 1017
Binghamton, NY 13902
(607) 778-5199

Chattanooga State Tech. Comm. College
Tisa Houck
Senior Library Assistant
4501 Amnicola Highway
Chattanooga, TN 37406
(615) 697-4400

Clackamas Community College
Cynthia R. Andrews
Director of Learning Resources Center
19600 South Molalla Avenue
Oregon City, OR 97045
(503) 657-6958

Cottey College
Rebecca Kiel
Assistant Library Director
1000 West Austin
Nevada, MO 64772
(417) 667-8187

Edmonds Community College
Greg Golden
Director of Learning Resources
20000 68th Avenue West
Lynnwood, WA 98036-5999
(206) 640-1522

Hillsborough Community College
Derrie B. Roark
Assoc. VP, Learning Resources
1502 East 9th Avenue
Tampa, FL 33605
(813) 253-7739

Kirkwood Community College
Jill Miller
Library Director
Box 2068
Cedar Rapids, IA 52406
(319) 398-5553

Kirtland Community College
Louise Bucco
Director of the Library
10775 North St. Helen Road
Roscommon, MI 48653
(517) 275-5121, ext. 235

Manatee Community College
Charles Kauderer
Director of Information Resources
Box 1849
Bradenton, FL 34206
(941) 755-1511, ext. 4254

Montgomery College
Connie Bakker
Campus Director, ESS
900 Hungerford Drive
Rockville, MD 20850-1733
(301) 650-1530

North Country Community College
Patrick F. McIntyre
Director of Libraries
20 Winona Avenue, Box 89
Saranac Lake, NY 12983
(518) 891-2915, ext. 222

Northwest Michigan College
Ronda Edwards
Director, Media & Distance Education
1701 East Front Street
Traverse City, MI 49686
(616) 922-1075

Pennsylvania College of Technology
Robert C. Johnston
Interim Library Director
One College Avenue
Williamsport, PA 17701-5778
(717) 327-4523

Pikes Peak Community College
Richard L. Friddle
Director of Learning Resources
5675 South Academy Boulevard
Colorado Springs, CO 80906-5498
(719) 540-7520

Pima County Community College
Robert K. Baker
Sr. Asst. to Vice Chancellor
   for Policy and Library Technology
4905C East Broadway Boulevard
Tucson, AZ 85709-1130
(520) 748-4989

Springfield Technical Community College
Lynn Kleindienst
Audiovisual Librarian
One Armory Square, Box 9000
Springfield, MA 01101
(413) 781-7822, ext. 3484

Tallahassee Community College
Mabel Shaw
Library Services Director
444 Appleyard Drive
Tallahassee, FL 32304-2895
(904) 922-8120

University of Colorado at Denver
Jean F. Hemphill
Assoc. Director for Administration,
   Auraria Library
Lawrence at 11th Street
Denver, CO 80204
(303) 556-2805

University of Maine at Augusta
Kirk T. Rau
Asst. Dean of Learning Resources
University Drive
Augusta, ME 04330-9410
(207) 621-3341

University of Toledo
Marcia Suter
Director of Learning Resources Center
2801 West Bancroft Street
Toledo, OH 43606
(419) 530-3175

William Rainey Harper College
Mary L. Severs
Technical Services Coordinator
1200 West Algonquin Road
Palatine, IL 60067
(847) 925-6000

BIBLIOGRAPHY

Becker, Gary H. Copyright: A Guide to Information and Resources. 1st Edition. Lake Mary, FL: Gary H. Becker, 1992.

       This day-to-day reference work for educators, librarians and media personnel introduces both traditional aspects of copyright as well as the law as it relates to newer technologies. Of special note are fair use situations and questions, sources of copyright cleared music and clip art, and sample ASCAP and BMI licensing agreements. Purchase includes permission for duplication and distribution for all or segments of this guide to the administration and staff at your institution.

Bielefield, Arlene, and Lawrence Cheeseman. Libraries & Copyright Law. New York: Neal-Schuman, 1993.

       This book discusses the copyright law's restrictions and privileges for the purpose of ensuring librarians take advantages of the special rights afforded them. Appended are required library copyright notices, excerpts from Congressional Report on Section 108, Copyright Remedy Clarification Act, and Computer Software Rental Amendment Act of 1989.

Brinson, J. Dianne, and Mark F. Radcliffe. Multimedia Law Handbook: A Practical Guide for Developers and Publishers. Menlo Park, CA: Ladera press, 1994.

       This work introduces the four intellectual property laws which affect multimedia developers (copyright, patent, trademark, and trade secret law) and includes eighteen sample agreements. Of special note are the sections on using preexisting works and obtaining licenses. It is endorsed by the Interactive Multimedia Association.

Bruwelheide, Janis H. The Copyright Primer for Librarians and Educators. Second Edition. Chicago: American Library Association, 1995.

       This concise overview of current copyright law and its interpretations focuses on the needs of educators and librarians. Special features include pragmatic question/answer sections, discussion of copyright and the newer technologies, copyright sites on the internet, and Sections 106-110 of the Copyright Law.

Dukelow, Ruth. The Library Copyright Guide. Washington, D.C.: Copyright Information Services, 1992.

       Written to help librarians, this work emphasizes permissible duplication of copyrighted materials made for library patrons, interlibrary loans, or internal use as covered under Section 108 of the Copyright Act. Acquisition permission to duplicate materials when copying does not fall under the protection of section 108 is also explained.

Elias, Stephen. <u>Patent, Copyright & Trademark: A Desk Reference to Intellectual Property Law</u>. Berkeley, CA: Nolo Press, 1996.
    Trade secret, copyright, patent, and trademark laws are introduced as they relate to intellectual property. Attorney Elias presents an overview, definitions, sample forms, and appropriate statutes in a ready reference format.

Gasaway, Laura N. and Sarah K. Wiant. <u>Libraries and Copyright: A Guide to Copyright Law in the 1990s</u>. Washington, D.C.: Special Libraries Association, 1994.
    Written for special librarians, this book focuses on the fundamentals of the copyright law and its application to traditional requests and on answers to questions about library uses of copyrighted works that have not yet been resolved. It also includes sections on international copyright and Canadian and British copyright law.

Goldstein, Paul. <u>Copyright's Highway: From Gutenberg to the Celestial Jukebox</u>. New York: Hill and Wang, 1994.
    This work discusses the evolution of legal and popular thought on copyright, including the concept of fair use. The author explores what steps might be necessary to ensure the newer technologies and intellectual freedom survive copyright.

Miller, Jerome K. <u>Applying the New Copyright Law: A Guide for Educators and Librarians</u>. Chicago: American Library Association, 1977.
    This classic work was written to help librarians and teachers understand the copyright law and to apply it to their work. Of special note are sections about fair use, library photocopying, and securing permissions.

Miller, Jerome K. et al. <u>Video Copyright Permissions: A Guide to Securing Permission to Retain, Perform, and Transmit Television Programs Videotaped Off the Air</u>. Friday Harbor, WA: Copyright Information Services, 1989.
    This book of readings summarizes the legal and ethical issues relating to television programs videotaped off the air and provides pragmatic suggestions for securing permissions to retain and use these programs. It also identifies public domain programming and discusses closed-circuit television system use.

Sinofsky, Esther R. <u>A Copyright Primer for Educational and Industrial Media Producers</u>. Second edition. Washington, D.C.: Copyright Information Services, 1994.
    Written for educators, industrial trainers, amateur and small producers, this work discusses key sections of the current copyright act and focuses on specific production-related issues. Of special interest are recent case studies, the Berne Convention, and clip art usage.

Talab, R. S. Copyright and Instructional Technologies: A Guide to Fair Use and Permissions Procedures. Second edition. Washington, D.C.: Association for Educational Communications and Technology, 1989.

 This document provides conservative and practical guidance for media and technology professionals as they seek to understand and comply with the intent and meaning of the copyright law. Included are a series of pragmatic application questions clarifying the fair use guidelines.

   . "Copyright, Legal, and Ethical Issues in the Internet Environment," Tech Trends. 39 (March 1994): 11-14.

 Copyright law, criminal law, and ethics are discussed as related to digital information networking. Specifically, the internet, electronic bulletin board systems, computer viruses, and public domain images, music, and copyright are topics included.

Vlcek, Charles W. Adoptable Copyright Policy: Copyright Policy and Manuals Designed for Adoption by Schools, Colleges, & Universities. Washington, D.C.: Copyright Information Services, 1992.

 Designed to help educational institutions establish a protective copyright policy, this book presents a model board policy and corresponding faculty and student copyright manuals. Of special note is the model "Copyright Quick Guide" summarizing copyright law for faculty.

Weil, Ben H., and Barbara F. Polansky. Modern Copyright Fundamentals: Key Writings on Technological and Other Issues. Revised edition. Medford, N.J.: Learned Information, 1989.

 Sponsored by ASIS, these readings include a model policy concerning photocopying for classroom, research, and reserve use, an off-air copying update, nonprint works and copyright, and more.

FAIR USE CRITERIA
AND
RELATED GUIDELINES

Section 107. Limitations on exclusive rights: Fair use

Notwithstanding the provisions of section 106 and 106A, the fair use of a copyrighted work, including such use by reproduction in copies or phonorecords or by any other means specified by that section, for purposes such as criticism, comment, news reporting, teaching (including multiple copies for classroom use, scholarship, or research, is not an infringement of copyright. In determining whether the use made of a work in any particular case is a fair use, the factors to be considered shall include--

(1) the purpose and character of the use, including whether such use is of a commercial nature or is for nonprofit educational purposes;

(2) the nature of the copyrighted work;

(3) the amount and substantiality of the portion used in relation to the copyrighted work as a whole; and

(4) the effect of the use upon the potential market for or value of the copyrighted work.

The fact that a work is unpublished shall not itself bar a finding of fair use if such finding is made upon consideration of all the above factors.

AGREEMENT ON GUIDELINES FOR
CLASSROOM COPYING
IN NOT-FOR-PROFIT EDUCATIONAL INSTITUTIONS
WITH RESPECT TO BOOKS AND PERIODICALS

The purpose of the following guidelines is to state the minimum standards of educational fair use under Section 107 of H.R. 2223. The parties agree that the conditions determining the extent of permissible copying for educational purposes may change in the future; that certain types of copying permitted under these guidelines may not be permissible in the future; and conversely that in the future other types of copying not permitted under these guidelines may be permissible under revised guidelines.

Moreover, the following statement of guidelines is not intended to limit the types of copying permitted under the standards of fair use under judicial decision and which are stated in Section 107 of the Copyright Revision Bill. There may be instances in which copying which does not fall within the guidelines stated below may nonetheless be permitted under the criteria of fair use.

GUIDELINES

I. *Single Copying for Teachers*
A single copy may be made of any of the following by or for a teacher at his or her individual request for his or her scholarly research or use in teaching or preparation to teach a class:
  A. A chapter from a book;
  B. An article from a periodical or newspaper;
  C. A short story, short essay or short poem, whether or not from a collective work;
  D. A chart, graph, diagram, drawing, cartoon or picture from a book, periodical, or newspaper.

II. *Multiple Copies for Classroom Use*
Multiple copies (not to exceed in any event more than one copy per pupil in a course) may be made by or for the teacher giving the course for classroom use or discussion; *provided that:*
  A. The copying meets the tests of brevity and spontaneity as defined below; *and,*
  B. Meets the cumulative effect test as defined below; *and,*
  C. Each copy includes a notice of copyright.

Definitions

Brevity

(i) Poetry: (a) A complete poem if less than 250 words and if printed on not more than two pages or, (b) from a longer poem, an excerpt of not more than 250 words.

(ii) Prose: (a) Either a complete article, story or essay of less than 2,500 words, or (b) an excerpt from any prose work of not more than 1,000 words or 10% of the work, whichever is less, but in any event a minimum of 500 words.

[Each of the numerical limits stated in "i" and "ii" above may be expanded to permit the completion of an unfinished line of a poem or of an unfinished prose paragraph.]

(iii) Illustration: One chart, graph, diagram, drawing, cartoon or picture per book or per periodical issue.

(iv) "Special" works: Certain works in poetry, prose or in "poetic prose" which often combine language with illustrations and which are intended sometimes for children and at other times for a more general audience fall short of 2,500 words in their entirety. Paragraph "ii" above notwithstanding such "special works" may not be reproduced in their entirety; however, an excerpt comprising not more than two of the published pages of such special work and containing not more than 10% of the words found in the text thereof, may be reproduced.

Spontaneity

(i) The copying is at the instance and inspiration of the individual teacher, and

(ii) The inspiration and decision to use the work and the moment of its use for maximum teaching effectiveness are so close in time that it would be unreasonable to expect a timely reply to a request for permission.

Cumulative Effect

(i) The copying of the material is for only one course in the school in which the copies are made.

(ii) Not more than one short poem, article, story, essay or two excerpts may be copied from the same author, nor more than three from the same collective work or periodical volume during one class term.

(iii) There shall not be more than nine instances of such multiple copying for one course during one class term.

[The limitations stated in "ii" and "iii" above shall not apply to current news periodicals and newspapers and current news sections of other periodicals.]

III. *Prohibitions as to I and II Above*

Notwithstanding any of the above, the following shall be prohibited:

(A) Copying shall not be used to create or to replace or substitute for anthologies, compilations or collective works. Such replacement or substitution may occur whether copies of various works or excerpts therefrom are accumulated or reproduced and used separately.

(B) There shall be no copying of or from works intended to be "consumable" in the course of study or of teaching. These include workbooks, exercises, standardized tests and test booklets and answer sheets and like consumable material.

(C) copying shall not:

(a) substitute for the purchase of books, publishers' reprints or periodicals;

(b) be directed by higher authority;

(c) be repeated with respect to the same item by the same teacher from term to term.

(D) No charge shall be made to the student beyond the actual cost of the photocopying.

Agreed MARCH 19, 1976.

Ad Hoc Committee on Copyright Law Revision:
                        By SHELDON ELLIOTT STEINBACH
Author-Publisher Group:

Authors League of America:
                        By IRWIN KARP, Counsel

Association of American Publishers, Inc.:
                        By ALEXANDER C. HOFFMAN,
                        Chairman, Copyright Committee

GUIDELINES FOR OFF-AIR RECORDING OF
BROADCAST PROGRAMMING
FOR EDUCATIONAL PURPOSES

In accordance with what we believe was (the) intent, the Negotiating Committee has limited its discussion to nonprofit educational institutions and to television programs broadcast for reception by the general public without charge. Within the guidelines, the Negotiating Committee does not intend that off-air recordings by teachers under fair use be permitted to be intentionally substituted in the school curriculum for a standard practice of purchase or license of the same educational material by the institution concerned.

1.   The guidelines were developed to apply only to off-air recordings by nonprofit educational institutions.

2.   A broadcast program may be recorded off-air simultaneously with broadcast transmission (including simultaneous cable retransmission) and retained by a nonprofit educational institution for a period not to exceed the first forty five (45) consecutive calendar days after date of recording. Upon conclusion of such retention period, all off-air recordings must be erased or destroyed immediately. "Broadcast programs" are television programs transmitted by television stations for reception by the general public without charge.

3.   Off-air recordings may be used once by individual teachers in the course of relevant teaching activities, and repeated once only when instructional reinforcement is necessary, in classrooms and similar places devoted to instruction within a single building, cluster or campus, as well as in the homes of students receiving formalized home instruction, during the first ten (10) consecutive school days in the forty-five (45) day calendar day retention period.

4.   Off-air recordings may be made only at the request of and used by individual teachers, and may not be regularly recorded in anticipation of requests. No broadcast program may be recorded off-air more than once at the request of the same teacher, regardless of the number of times the program may be broadcast.

5.   A limited number of copies may be reproduced from each off-air recording to meet the legitimate needs of teachers under these guidelines. Each such additional copy shall be subject to all provisions governing the original recording.

6. After the first ten (10) consecutive school days, off-air recordings may be used up to the end of the forty-five (45) calendar day retention period only for teacher evaluation purposes, i.e. to determine whether or not to include the broadcast program in the teaching curriculum, and may not be used in the recording institution for student exhibition or any other nonevaluation purpose without authorization.

7. Off-air recordings need not be used in their entirety, but the recorded programs may not be altered from their original content. Off-air recordings may not be physically or electronically combined or merged to constitute teaching anthologies or compilations.

8. All copies of off-air recordings must include the copyright notice on the broadcast program as recorded.

9. Educational institutions are expected to establish appropriate control procedures to maintain the integrity of these guidelines.

1987 STATEMENT ON SOFTWARE COPYRIGHT:
AN ICCE POLICY STATEMENT

Background

During 1982-83, educators, software developers, and hardware and software vendors cooperated to develop the *ICCE Policy Statement on Network and Multiple Machine Software.* This Policy Statement was adopted by the Board of Directors of the International Council for Computers in Education (ICCE), in 1983, and was published and distributed. It has received support from hardware and software vendors, industry associations and other education associations. One component of the Policy Statement, the "Model District Policy on Software Copyright," has been adopted by school districts throughout the world.

Now, three years later, as the educational computer market has changed and the software market has matured, ICCE has responded to suggestions that the policy statement be reviewed by a new committee and revisions be made to reflect the changes that have taken place both in the market place and in the schools.

The 1986-87 ICCE Software Copyright Committee is composed of educators, industry associations, hardware vendors, software developers and vendors, and lawyers. All the participants of this new Committee agree that the educational market should be served by developers and preserved by educators. To do so requires that the ICCE Policy Statement be revisited every few years while the industry and the use of computers in education are still developing.

Responsibilities

In the previous Policy Statement, lists of responsibilities were assigned to appropriate groups: educators; hardware vendors; and software developers and vendors. The suggestion that school boards show their responsibility by approving a district copyright policy was met with enthusiasm, and many districts approved a policy based on the ICCE Model Policy. The suggestion that software vendors adopt multiple-copy discounts and offer lab packs to schools was likewise well received; many educational software publishers now offer such pricing. It is therefore the opinion of this committee that, for the most part, the 1983 list of recommendations has become a fait accompli within the industry, and to repeat it here would be an unnecessary redundancy.

Nevertheless, the Committee does suggest that all parties involved in the educational computing market be aware of what the other parties are doing to preserve this market, and that the following three recommendations be considered for adoption by the appropriate agencies.

School District Copyright Policy

The Committee recommends that school districts approve a District Copyright Policy that includes both computer software and other media. A Model District Policy on Software Copyright is enclosed.

Particular attention should be directed to item five, recommending that *only one* person in the district be given the authority to sign software licensing agreements. This implies that such a person should become familiar with licensing and purchasing rights of all copyrighted materials.

Suggested Software Use Guidelines

In the absence of clear legislation, legal opinion or case law, it is suggested that school districts adopt the enclosed Suggested Software Use Guidelines as guidelines for software use within the district. The recommendation of Guidelines is similar to the situation currently used by many education agencies for off-air video recording. While these Guidelines do not carry the force of law, they do represent the collected opinion on fair software use for nonprofit education agencies from a variety of experts in the software copyright field.

Copyright Page Recommendations

The Committee recommends that educators look to the copyright page of software documentation to find their rights, obligations and license restrictions regarding an individual piece of software.

The Committee also suggests that software publishers use the documentation copyright page to *clearly* delineate the users' (owners' or licensees') rights in at least these five areas:

1.   How is a back-up copy made or obtained, how many are allowed, and how are the back-ups to be used (e.g., not to be used on a second machine at the same time)?

2.   Is it permissible to load the disk(s) into multiple computers for use at the same time?

3.   Is it permissible to use the software on a local area network, and will the company support such use? Or is a network version available from the publisher?

4.   Are lab packs or quantity discounts available from the publisher?

5.   Is it permissible for the owner or licensee to make copies of the printed documentation? or are additional copies available, and how?

ICCE -- Suggested Software Use Guidelines

The 1976 U.S. Copyright Act and its 1980 Amendments remain vague in some areas of software use and its application to education. Where the law itself is vague. software licenses tend to be much more specific. It is therefore imperative that educators read the software's copyright page and understand the licensing restrictions printed there. If these uses are not addressed, the following Guidelines are recommended.

These Guidelines do not have the force of law, but they do represent the collected opinion on fair software use by nonprofit educational agencies from a variety of experts in the software copyright field.

Back-up Copy: The Copyright Act is clear in permitting the owner of software a back-up copy of the software to be held for use as an archival copy in the event the original disk fails to function. Such back-up copies are not to be used on a second computer at the same time the original is in use.

Multiple-loading: The Copyright Act is most unclear as it applies to loading the contents of one disk into multiple computers for use at the same time. In the absence of a license expressly permitting the user to load the contents of one disk into many computers for use at the same time, it is suggested that you not allow this activity to take place. The fact that you physically can do so is irrelevant. In an effort to make it easier for schools to buy software for each computer station, many software publishers offer lab packs and other quantity buying incentives. Contact individual publishers for details.

Local Area Network Software Use: It is suggested that before placing a software program on a local area network or disk-sharing system for use by multiple users at the same time, you obtain a written license agreement from the copyright holder giving you permission to do so. The fact that you are able to physically load the program on the network is, again, irrelevant. You should obtain a license permitting you to do so before you act.

Model District Policy on Software Copyright

It is the intent of [district] to adhere to the provisions of copyright laws in the area of microcomputer software. It is also the intent of the district to comply with the license agreements and/or policy statements contained in the software packages used in the district. In circumstances where the interpretation of the copyright law is ambiguous, the district shall look to the applicable license agreement to determine appropriate use of the software (or the district will abide by the approved Software Use guidelines).

We recognize that computer software piracy is a major problem for the industry and that violations of copyright laws contribute to higher costs and greater efforts to prevent copying and/or lessen incentives for the development of effective educational uses of microcomputers. Therefore, in an effort to discourage violation of copyright laws and to prevent such illegal activities:

1.   The ethical and practical implications of software piracy will be taught to educators and school children in all schools in the district (e.g., covered in fifth grade social studies classes).

2.   District employees will be informed that they are expected to adhere to section 117 of the 1976 Copyright Act as amended in 1980, governing the use of software (e.g., each building principal will devote one faculty meeting to the subject each year).

3.   When permission is obtained from the copyright holder to use software on a disk-sharing system, efforts will be made to secure this software from copying.

4.   Under no circumstances shall illegal copies of copyrighted software be made or used on school equipment.

5.   [Name or job title] of this school district is designated as the only individual who may sign license agreements for software for schools in the district. Each school using licensed software should have a signed copy of the software agreement.

6.   The principal at each school site is responsible for establishing practices which will enforce this district copyright policy at the school level.

The Board of Directors of the International Council for Computers in Education approved this policy statement January, 1987. The members of the 1986 ICCE Software Copyright Committee are:
        Sueann Ambron, American Association of Publishers
        Gary Becker, Seminole County Public Schools, Florida
        Daniel T. Brooks, Cadwalader, Wickersham & Taft
        LeRoy Finkel, International Council for Computers in Education
        Virginia Helm, Western Illinois University
        Kent Kehrberg, Minnesota Educational Computing Corporation
        Dan Kunz, Commodore Business Machines
        Bodie Marx, Mindscape, Inc.
        Kenton Pattie, International Communications Industries Association
        Carol Risher, American Association of Publishers
        Linda Roberts, U.S. Congress, Office of Technology Assessment
        Donald A. Ross, Microcomputer Workshops Courseware
        Lary Smith, Wayne County Intermediate School District, Michigan
        Ken Wasch, Software Publishers Association

For more information write to the ICCE Software Copyright Committee, ICCE, University of Oregon, 1787 Agade Street, Eugene, OR 97403

PUBLIC LAW 96-517 (COMPUTER AMENDMENT)
DECEMBER 12, 1980
Copyright Law Amended Regarding Computer Programs

The following excerpt amending title 17, United States Code, is taken from Public Law 96-517, dated December 12, 1980 (94 Stat. 3028-29).

Sec. 10. (a) Section 102 of title 17 of the United States Code is amended to add at the end thereof the following new language:

"A 'computer program' is a set of statements or instructions to be used directly or indirectly in a computer in order to bring about a certain result."

(b) Section 117 of title 17 of the United States Code is amended to read as follows:

"§117. Limitations on exclusive rights: Computer programs

"Notwithstanding the provisions of section 106, it is not an infringement for the owner of a copy of a computer program to make or authorize the making" of another copy or adaptation of that computer program provided:

"(1) that such a new copy or adaptation is created as an essential step in the utilization of the computer program in conjunction with a machine and that is used in no other manner, or

"(2) that such new copy or adaptation is for archival purposes only and that all archival copies are destroyed in the event that continued possession of the computer program should cease to be rightful.

"Any exact copies prepared in accordance with the provisions of this section may be leased, sold, or otherwise transferred, along with the copy from which such copies were prepared, only as part of the lease, sale, or other transfer of all rights in the program. Adaptations so prepared may be transferred only with the authorization of the copyright owner."

GUIDELINES FOR EDUCATIONAL USES OF MUSIC

The purpose of the following guidelines is to state the minimum and not the maximum standards of educational fair use under Section 107 of HR2223. The parties agree that the conditions determining the extent of permissible copying for educational purposes may change in the future, that certain types of copying permitted under these guidelines may not be permissible in the future, and conversely that in the future other types of copying which are not permitted under these guidelines may be permissible under revised guidelines. Moreover, the following statement of guidelines is not intended to limit the types of copying permitted under the standards of fair use under judicial decision and which are stated in Section 107 of the Copyright Revision Bill. There may be instances in which copying which does not fall within the guidelines stated below may nonetheless be permitted under the criteria of fair use.

A. *Permissible Uses*

1. Emergency copying to replace purchased copies which for any reason are not available for any imminent performance provided purchased replacement copies shall be substituted in due course.

2. (a) [amended} For academic purposes other than performance, single or multiple copies of excerpts of works may be made, provided that the excerpts do not comprise a part of the whole which would constitute a performable unit such as a section, movement or aria, but in no case more than 10% of the whole work. The number of copies shall not exceed one copy per pupil.

(b) For academic purposes other than performance, a single copy of an entire performable unit (section, movement, aria, etc.) that is, (1) confirmed by the copyright proprietor to be out of print or (2) unavailable except in a larger work, may be made by or for a teacher solely for the purpose of his or her scholarly research or in preparation to teach a class.

3. Printed copies which have been purchased may be edited or simplified provided that the fundamental character of the work is not distorted or the lyrics, if any, altered or lyrics added if none exist.

4. A single copy of recordings of performances by students may be made for evaluation or rehearsal purposes and may be retained by the educational institution or individual teacher.

5. A single copy of a sound recording (such as a tape, disc, or cassette) of copyrighted music may be made from sound recordings owned by an educational institution or an individual teacher for the purpose of constructing aural exercises or examinations and may be retained by the educational institution or individual teacher. (This pertains only to the copyright of the music itself and not to any copyright which may exist in the sound recording.)

B. *Prohibitions*

1. Copying to create or replace or substitute for anthologies, compilations or collective works.

2. Copying of or from works intended to be "consumable" in the course of study or of teaching such as workbooks, exercises, standardized tests and answer sheets and like material.

3. Copying for the purpose of performance, except as in A(1) above.

4. Copying for the purpose of substituting for the purchase of music, except as in A(1) and A(2) above.

5. Copying without inclusion of the copyright notice which appears on the printed copy.

THE NATIONAL COMMISSION ON THE NEW TECHNOLOGICAL USES OF COPYRIGHTED WORKS (CONTU) GUIDELINES FOR THE PROVISO OF SUBSECTION 108(g)(2) FOR INTERLIBRARY LOANS

1.   As used in the proviso of subsection 108(g)(2), the words, "... such aggregate quantities as to substitute for a subscription or purchase of such work" shall mean:

(a)   With respect to any given periodical (as opposed to any given issue of a periodical), filled requests of a library or archived (a "requesting entity") within any calendar year for a total of six or more copies of an article or articles published in such periodical within five years prior to the date of the request. These guidelines specifically shall not apply, directly or indirectly, to any request of a requesting entity for a copy or copies of an article or articles published in any issue of a periodical, the publication date of which is more than five years prior to the date when the request was made. These guidelines do not define the meaning, with respect to such a request, of "...such aggregate quantities as to substitute for a subscription to (such periodical)"

(b)   With respect to any other material described in subsection 108(d), (including fiction or poetry), filled requests of a requesting entity within any calendar year for a total of six or more copies of phonorecords or from any given work (including a collective work) during the entire period when such material shall be protected by copyright.

2.   In the event that a requesting entity

(a)   shall have in force or shall have entered an order for a subscription to a periodical, or

(b)   has within its collection, or shall have entered an order for a copy or phonorecord of any other copyrighted work, material from either category of which it desires to obtain by copy from another library or archives (the "supplying entity"), because the material to be copied is not reasonably available for use by the requesting entity itself, then the fulfillment of such request shall be treated as though the requesting entity made such copy from its own collection. A library or archives may request a copy or phonorecord from a supplying entity only under those circumstances where the requesting entity would have been able, under the provisions of section 108, to supply such copy from materials in its own collection.

3.   No request for a copy or phonorecord of any material to which these guidelines apply may be fulfilled by the supplying entity unless such request is accompanied by a representation by the requesting entity that the request was made in conformity with these guidelines.

4.   The requesting entity shall maintain records of all requests made by it for copies or phonorecords of any materials to which these guidelines apply and shall maintain records of the fulfillment of such requests, which records shall be retained until the end of the third complete calendar year after the end of the calendar year in which the respective request shall have been made.

5.   As part of the review provided for in subsection 108(I), these guidelines shall be reviewed not later than five years from the effective date of this bill.

ABOUT THE EDITORS AND SECTION

Wanda K. Johnston (MALS, Rosary College) is Director of Learning Resources, Central Florida Community College. She has over twenty years of experience with both liberal arts and community college library/learning resources programs. She has served on and chaired numerous committees of the Association of Educational Communications and Technology, Association of College and Research Libraries, and more. She has written a variety of articles on information technology, library instruction, needs assessment and program development. She recently authored <u>Administering the Community College Learning Resources Program</u>.

Derrie B. Roark (Ed.D, Florida State University; MLS, Louisiana State University) is the Associate Vice President of Learning Resources Services, Hillsborough Community College. She has twenty years experience in community college learning resources services, with additional experience in university, college, and public libraries. She has chaired ACRL/CJCLS, the National Council of Learning Resources, the Florida ACRL Chapter, the Florida CCLA Advisory Board, and is currently chair of the Board of the Tampa Bay Library Consortium and President of the Board of the Tampa Educational Cable Consortium. She has authored several articles or chapters and is an adjunct faculty member of the graduate Library and Information Science Program of the University of South Florida.

The Community and Junior College Libraries Section, an active section of the Association of College and Research Libraries (ALA), has as its mission to contribute to library service and librarianship through activities that relate to libraries and learning resources centers that support the educational programs in community and junior colleges and equivalent institutions. This goal is implemented by more than a dozen standing and ad hoc committees reflecting the interests and activities of section members. The section supports awards, conference programs, and publishing ventures such as this volume.

INDEX